To find more by this author,
please log onto:

http://www.funsub.com

Mark Crane

Love, Actually
Realizing the Universal Loving Ideal

Library of Congress Cataloging-in-Publication Data

Crane, Mark T.

   Love, Actually: Realizing the Universal Loving Ideal/by Mark Crane.-- 1st ed.

ISBN 978-1-105-82963-5

Love, Actually
Realizing the Universal Loving Ideal

Keep an open mind, and I promise I will not lead you somewhere you've been before.

Mark Crane, New York City, 6/27/2012.

Chapter One
A Turning Point

Shall not the Judge of all the earth do what is just?
- Genesis, 18:25

Sister George Mary stood at the front of the room facing us, and we were composed, our eyes set on the oak door, impossible to see much in the dark hallway at this angle through the gray square of safety glass. The pastor of our church was about to enter the room, and I was prepared for great revelations.

Although I knew him already.

I could say I knew him better than any of the others- since I was an altar boy and I'd been through plenty of Sunday masses at his side- but there really wasn't much to know. Priests entered the sacristy in a sort of a zone, and they rarely would call you by name, let alone get into any conversation that wasn't about the ritual you were about to produce. Unlike my father, who was open and engaging with me, priests seemed to me to be inward men, with perhaps a great store of anger deep below, that being the best reason I could figure for why their personalities were stony and dry. It was my understanding that devout Catholics like priests saved their emotional side for intensely private moments with intimate confidantes- maybe other priests, close family members.

The truth was I knew nothing about Father Bradley the other kids didn't. I saw the same thing they did on Sunday mornings, just from a side view.

It was Media, Pennsylvania, a county seat, a nice balance between town and city- leafy, but all sidewalked, and busy, with a distinct main street- State Street- that featured a trolley from Philadelphia running right up the center.

We had been told that now that we'd reached the eighth grade, Father Bradley was making a special trip the two blocks over from the rectory to visit our classroom. We would get to meet him, "for a talk," Sister George had said.

Religion was central to my life. Since my parents had wanted to enter me into school early- something only the public schools would allow- I'd been unable to follow my three older brothers into Catholic school. At the dinner table, much conversation would swirl above and beyond me. Even my mother, who taught third grade at a nearby Catholic school, would be able to put a face and character to the names that animated my brothers' stories.

Then, in the 7th Grade, I'd finally been admitted, and I was so happy to dive into the culture I'd only dipped my toes into Sunday mornings or in the few weeks of preparation for my First Holy Communion.

There were depths to my religion I was eager to explore.

There was, of course, the sacrament of that part of life- confirmation. And I picked up being an altar boy as eagerly as I inherited the paper route that each of my brothers had run before me. I even joined the Legion of Mary, a group of especially devout Catholics who focused their efforts at prayer as a group, a group that you joined out of zeal for your faith. We spent many hours being instructed by the nuns and lay volunteers on the stories of the saints and the variety of devotions we would practice. We would take trips to the local nursing home to pray with lonely, ancient remnants of the turn of the century, once children who had danced around May poles and run with hoops.

My devotion filled my mind with important questions.

It was possible, I understood, that Father Bradley would do something along the lines of what he was doing in church every week. He might pray or bless us. I guess I wouldn't have been surprised to see him pull out a shaker of holy water and give us all a sprinkle. Maybe he would lecture, the way he did in his homily, which I assumed only adults could really understand, as I never did. The homily was like listening to the news- there were too many words and references I couldn't understand, and no matter how I tried, my only way to stay still was to get my mind to drift to something that could entertain a kid. I would try to keep it holy, letting my eyes roam to the Stations of the Cross along the wall and my thoughts to the dramatic drama of Jesus's crucifixion. Or maybe I'd try to make some sense of the stained glass images of buxom, haloed ladies and portly cherubs.

Or my eyes might find a girl looking in my direction, and I'd wonder if she was noticing and might be impressed by my serious poise. Or I'd see a piece of molding that ran along the balcony that looked like an upside-down cross, a menacing reminder that evil was nearby always, and that I must be on guard. If I could only understand what the priest was talking about.

Maybe that was the problem. Ideas like redemption and mercy and sacrifice were out of my young mind's reach, and rather than studiously pulling them in, I was comfortable with finding a way to live outside them. It wasn't like the *adults* were very interested in the homilies. Many adults would fall asleep. And what a clear expression of relief would be seen from the adults at the end of the homily- not just from me. I never heard anyone on the church steps talking about redemption or mercy or sacrifice. It was my understanding (though I never gave it a moment's thought) that the adults were just much better than me at enduring the homily, and that endurance of tedious ritual was as Christian as Christ's own suffering trials. I would force myself to kneel perfectly erect, while my gaze surveyed the congregants for other such erect kneelers, telling myself that they were clearly the most devout.

So it was entirely possible Father Bradley would bore us all with incomprehensibles.

It was also possible he had something special to reveal- secrets that would change the course of my life. I was ready to be guided entirely by....

- I was not, I think, ready to be guided blindly by instruction from priests or nuns. I was not ready even to be guided by biblical edicts-

What I was ready for was to be animated by what my religion revealed to me was righteous. What felt right to me was not that I should follow any instruction, but that I should find something within me that would help me understand what I must do.

I yearned for that.

Father Bradley came through the door. The Mother Superior in the hall only advanced as far as the doorway, and Sister George, a broad-shouldered and muscular woman of German stock- a woman who was adept at removing the humor from situations with a crack of her palm to the back of a young head- took herself quietly to the rear of the room.

He sat on the edge of a desk. That was the effect he sought. He began with a little quiet small talk, some chit-chat - friendly, "how's-everything-going" kind of stuff- which was already a let-down because his demeanor suggested he had nothing planned. This was a visit, simply.

Then, he took a barely-audible cleansing breath, like he might get up and walk out the door, and just as soon, his voice started low, at almost a murmur, calmly running off a game plan for us. We would be good Catholic children. We would respect our parents. He was confident we would keep our sacraments alive, and, wherever life took us, we would keep Jesus in our hearts. It was the tone of voice you heard from a priest in the confessional: soft, a little bored, like these are all things that have previously been discussed. He was recapping for us. These were things that were so vital we simply had to be all too well aware of them.

Then he rubbed his palms on the thighs of his slacks, leaned forward, and asked if we had any questions.

After we shifted a bit in our seats, Sister George's voice pronounced an oddly moderated encouragement to speak up and ask anything, truly anything at all that might cause us confusion about our religion or really any questions about life, revealing that the nature of this forum had been deliberated upon more than it had at first seemed.

"Does God love Satan?" asked Cynthia, a sycophantic teacher's pet.

"What is Hell like?" asked Steve, a kid with a concentrated interest in the more dangerous aspects of most topics.

"How old is it normal for girls and boys to fall in love?" asked Cathy, who was picking up on the thread of possibility that maybe they were looking for questions related to our maturation.

As these questions were being asked and answered, my mind was seeking an important question, one that would wake a few dogs, something at the heart of religious mystery. There were no hands but mine next and he called on me.

My thinking continued on my feet. "Let's saaaay there is a person who doesn't believe in God, buuuuut who does all he can to be very good. Let's say he spends all his life helping people, and then dies. Would God still send him to hell?"

I wasn't trying to start trouble. I probably hadn't even considered the possibility that there was not a good answer to my question, that my puny thoughts could threaten the core beliefs of people like this priest and nun. And maybe it wasn't just logic bothering me but the fact that my dear father was not faithful enough to stand the tests these people outlined (I wouldn't be interested in going to heaven if he wasn't there.) I don't know, but for some reason I could not make the leap between a selfless, charitable Jesus and a God who was so interested in getting credit that he would damn a perfectly moral person for eternity just because that person did not believe in God.

My father would always mock my grandmother and great aunts for their servility to the church, its priests, and edicts. You shouldn't fear religion. And wasn't Jesus's message that you shouldn't fear God?

Well, maybe not. His message was more like you shouldn't fear Jesus.

But Jesus and God, these confounding teachers drilled into us, are the same thing.

I did not look back at Sister George, though I could hear exasperation in her breathing. Father Bradley looked away, where he might compose his reply in private. His eyebrows slightly twisted then, and he blinked a few times before returning a humored gaze in my direction. Not one kid made a sound.

"There are two theories on that," he replied, very calmly. "Either the man will go to Hell, just because he does not believe-because God *does* command us to believe. Or he goes to Hell because he is not really good, since no one who fails to believe could *really* do good things for what is actually, deep in his soul, a good reason." His smile was thin and he did not let his eyes stay on me a moment longer before rising up, leading us all in an Our Father, then drawing from his large cassock pocket a holy water shaker. He uncapped it and gave us a generous sprinkling before walking out the door.

That was the first moment I felt truly let down by my religion. Looking back, I see the issue at heart was the contradiction between my own ideals and those of my religion's God.

If a God behaves in an unloving way, should we follow? Let's say a religion we espouse leads us to commit acts we believe to be immoral. Or perhaps we are merely called on to follow a passively immoral holy leader, like one who has allowed children to be victimized as we've recently seen with the Catholic clergy child rape scandals where bishops transferred child molesting priests from parish-to-parish, secretly exposing new victims to them- or one who fails to lead his congregation to oppose a swelling of immorality taking over the community- such as what happened throughout Rwanda in the days leading up to the genocide- or really in any nation getting enthused over the prospect of an unnecessary slaughter or brutality of any kind. Do we follow a religious leader like that?

It either is or it isn't proper for us to question the leaders of our religion, and, if we should scrutinize them, no small dose will suffice. Either these are angels walking the Earth or these are individuals capable of every flaw on the books. And you can't judge their religious counsel without investigating your religion enough to be a proper judge.

And that makes you a judge of the development of the history of that religion. Religions are not born of whole cloth. They are woven over centuries by active individuals, each of whom either are or are not deserving of scrutiny.

Are we sheep, as my religion always encouraged me to believe? Should we follow any religion we find ourselves born into, no matter what sort of radical or effete character it has? If we are not sheep- if we are instead to hold ourselves morally accountable for our religious decisions- we are not only in a position to judge the religions we follow, but it is our duty to do so.

Once it is our duty to question one small niche of our religion, the consequences are monumental- we are compelled to judge our religion and its, or *our,* concept of God with complete scrutiny.

And that can be a very difficult thing to do. When congregants begin to see themselves as the seeds rather than the fruit of a religion, the burden of such a responsibility can seem daunting, and only with great courage and faith can they be expected to complete the work that scrutiny requires.

Change obliges a settled person to become unsettled, to accept that all that has gone before them was never actually finished- to discover the ground under their feet is not dead, but *alive*; and that the work they've been led to believe merely requires obedient abidance has in fact been egregiously neglected.

This is *not* a notion of faith that doesn't connect with human experience enough to keep a congregation awake, but one that emanates *from* human experience. It is a faith residing within us that we are reminded of or have our attention called to, not one that is doled out to us in packets of mystery.

Radically, this new faith will release the struggle towards our loving ideals from the narrow confines of religious identity, and it will allow morality a universal expanse, a great victory for the most universal of religious ideals, the ideal of love.

Chapter Two

The Friendly Ghost Is Dead

"Why do you doubt your senses?"
"Because," said Scrooge, "a little thing affects them. A slight
disorder of the stomach makes them cheats. You may be an
undigested bit of beef, a blot of mustard, a crumb of cheese, a
fragment of an underdone potato. There's more of gravy than of
grave about you, whatever you are!"
- Charles Dickens's <u>A Christmas Carol</u>.

I told him, too, that he being in other things such an extremely
sensible and sagacious savage, it pained me, very badly pained
me, to see him now so deplorably foolish about this ridiculous
Ramadan of his. Besides, argued I, fasting makes the body cave
in; hence the spirit caves in; and all thoughts born of a fast must
necessarily be half-starved. This is the reason why most
dyspeptic religionists cherish such melancholy notions about
their hereafters. In one word, Queequeg, said I, rather
digressively; hell is an idea first born on an undigested apple-
dumpling; and since then perpetuated through the hereditary
dyspepsias nurtured by Ramadans.
- Herman Melville's <u>Moby Dick.</u>

There are not a whole lot of people in the world who were moved
to religious devotion through a study of science. On the contrary,
science has continuously withered religion's claims.

The latest scientific insight that seems to contradict
religion is perhaps more damaging than both the 16th century

Copernican revolution, which destroyed the Earth-centered universe concept, and the 18th and 19th century advances in understanding evolution, which, accompanied by an extensive fossil record, turned the book of Genesis on its ear.

Discoveries into the true nature of the human brain threaten to project religion farther yet out into the universe of ethereal mystery.

Imagine an android-type of creature- a computerized brain atop a body made of synthesized or recycled body parts so sophisticated that it can perform every task necessary to make it indistinguishable from a human (ie: *Star Trek*'s "Data" character.) Or, imagine a robotic creature with nothing but a real human brain running the show. More challenging yet, try on a computerized helmet of artificial quantum neurons that multiplies your brainpower a hundredfold, and then imagine "phasing out" your own tired neurons one-by-one over the next twenty years or so.

Don't say it won't be done. They already have biomedical prostheses that rewire the brain and interact with it by sending outside stimuli in wirelessly for help with a variety of malfunctions, from vision problems to Parkinson's disease, paralysis, epilepsy, and other human cognitive and sensory malfunctions.[1] The New York Times recently reported on a memory implant in rats that can record neural firing patterns and then refire them later to recreate memories, "...like a melody on a player piano."[2]

Now, I'd like you to consider the people who, due to brain damage, cannot remember their own mothers or their own childhood. And there are otherwise healthy people who cannot remember anything at all of what happens to them from one moment to the next.

Parts of the brain governing memory retrieval or storage can be damaged. The actual area where the memory is stored can be damaged.

If you take away your memories, are you still you?

My brain is where "I" am located, and it is (*I am*) an interconnection of physical neurons. Neurons are unimaginably

---

[1] For source/more info, see: http://ccnmtl.columbia.edu/projects/neuroethics/module4/foundationtext/index.html

[2] Carey, Benedict. "Memory Implant Gives Rats Sharper Recollection." New York Times, June 17, 2011.

tiny cells that get excited when they receive electricity and which respond by sending out electrical pulses. Each are structured essentially the same as the neurons of a fruit fly, with 10,000 synaptic connections each, but amassed to an incomprehensible 100 billion individual neurons in each human brain. Small groups of these neurons are essential to who I am, as, for instance, I would be horrified at the threat of losing the memory of my mother. And they are just as *unessential* to who I *will be*. I would not miss my mother's memory once it was stripped away, as you can't miss something you are unaware of. So each brain state in each piece of time lives its own independent existence. It is as if the present and future only *appear* to me to be a continuum, but are, in fact, unrelated strangers, just as disconnected as my first moment of early childhood cognizance from the moment that preceded it.

Let's say we take those 10,000 connections and multiply them by 100 billion. We get an extremely large number, a number big enough to control myriad physical and cognitive functions. And as our body is using these neurons to breathe, grow, pump blood, regulate how blood is pumped, operate and regulate all our other organs, think, remember, monitor our safety, balance... - I could go on all day listing in detail all the things the human body is doing- as all those neurons are running the show, I can still spare enough neuronal activity to coordinate my hand movement, so that it twists, not just up and down and from side to side like a robot, but in a graceful sweep, gesturing with each finger playing a different role, as I play a piano.

That incredibly large number allows incredible diversity, but it is also limited. I cannot beat a computer at chess. I cannot always remember where I left my glasses. I cannot write a message to one person simultaneously as I converse with another.

A good understanding of cognition, as a string of moments that exist independently from one to the other, with its vitality engaged in stored memories, takes apart our notion of identity.

The "spirit" I was raised to believe in- the one they taught me merely inhabited my body, invisibly, like Casper the Friendly Ghost- a spirit that I understood included my thoughts and memories- that spirit was invulnerable to the physical world. But a well-informed understanding of the brain presents the person I once regarded as my spirit as having a very physically vulnerable nature.

Over the last 30 years, science has been regularly defining the physical nature of phenomena once thought to be spiritual. Physical manipulation of the brain has been shown to be capable of producing feelings from déjà vu to pleasure, to anger or fear, and expressions like pouting, ardor, and surprise[3].

I'll offer you a very good example. Over the last decade, one of the favorite last hold-outs of spirituality-sponsored scientific confusion has been soundly dispelled. In 2002, electrical stimulation of the brains of certain epileptics was shown to induce the illusory perception known as "out-of-body experience."[4] In August, 2007, Swedish Neuroscientist, H. Henrik Ehrsson working then at the Institute of Neurology at University College of London produced the same experience in healthy subjects using merely *external* stimuli.[5]

Those operation-room testimonials of people's spirits rising to the ceiling before being yanked back have actually been consistent with the brain's inner workings. These are visual illusions called up by the confused misfunctioning of a rarely-discussed sense called "proprioception."

The brain is capable of imaging a variety of views from or of its body, (especially on the operating table when you're under deep sedation and someone's digging around in your chest, stimulating internal nerves in ways you've never experienced before.) Vision is not an inner "you" viewing a video simulcast from your optical nerves. Rather, our eyeballs provide electrical impulses- *electrical impulses*, nothing more- to our brain, and our brain integrates that data with much other sensory data to create a neural experience we call vision. We get depth of field, for example, by comparing data from each eye, aided by a sound map provided by our ears. Our experience only *seems* like a proper picture to us.

[3] Fish DR, Gloor P, Quesney FL, Olivier A (1993) Clinical responses to electrical brain stimulation of the temporal and frontal lobes in patients with epilepsy. Pathophysiological implications. Brain 116:397–414.
For source/more info, see:
http://brain.oxfordjournals.org/content/116/2/397.full.pdf
http://www.sciencedaily.com/releases/2008/01/080130092102.htm
[4] For source/more info, see: http://primal-page.com/penfield.htm
[5] For source/more info, see:
http://www.cosmosmagazine.com/news/1547/out-body-experiences-created-lab

Blind adults who have never seen may be able to gain perfectly-working eyes, but their brain, having already organized its neuronal networks without those functioning eyes, is incapable of making a useful picture from the data. In May of 2008, California Institute of Technology researchers published a study showing that people who, after having developed neuronal networks as sighted children and then losing their sight for many years due to disease or accident, actually have reorganized their use of neurons, so that, after regaining functioning eyes with new technologies as adults, even with two years therapy they can only interpret signals from their functoning eyes as shapes and blobs at best.[6]

Our brain cobbles sensory information into what we experience, the same way it recalls sensory info from memories to produce vivid dreams or illusive sensations, so believable, they are spookily labeled, "astral projection" and "spirit walking."

Despite what we were taught in school, we have more than five senses. Balance, makes six. Then there's pain and the movement of internal organs. And then there is proprioception.

Proprioception is your sense of where your body is in space, or, maybe more accurately, where you are in your body. It is the sense that tells you to duck your head when you are passing through a doorway with a tall hat. Our feeling of place in our body is just an illusion of integrity ...and an illusion of separateness at times, too.

Look at this illusion:

---

[6] For source/more info, see: http://media.caltech.edu/press_releases/13144

Your brain is telling you there are grey dots where the white lines meet, though there are not.

Like an optical illusion, out-of-body experience is a flaw in the brain's function, not supernatural phenomena. So, when an emergency room physician who is tired of hearing stories of people floating on the ceiling puts an ace-of-spades face-up on a high shelf in the ER, (just like when you cover over one row of black squares in the preceding illustration,) they can debunk the spookiness and provide us a glimpse into the brain's ever-active creativity.

It is more obvious than you might suspect. You can kind of do it right now: Imagine your body becoming weightless, and imagine watching from your eyes as your floating body turns in the air to face the floor, and then feel yourself float to the ceiling. Sure, there's no visual sensation, but the information is all there. You know where the chair is. You know just what it looks like as you rise up, looking down on it. You even know what the weightlessness would feel like- like it felt the first time your father tossed you in the air as a child. (And who hasn't experienced weightlessness vividly already in a dream?)

Of course, we could say there are still mysteries embedded in brain science, but each such "mystery" would be better labeled a "not-yet known," as it seems reasonable to expect anything our brains do to eventually be revealed as attributable to natural law and subject to the confines of an organic, mortal anatomy- from reading to processing thoughts and memories, yearning, or hurting.

For instance, let's say we say about an acquaintance: "That person has a spirit that is..." (let's think up a good one here- a trait that seems very disembodied,) "...*loving*."

First, we know how the brain can be manipulated to cheer people up. Once when I was working at a job where it was my responsibility to move trains around a railroad yard, I met the nastiest, meanest, most irrationally irritable dispatcher that surely ever existed on Earth. (No, really.) It was my first month on the job, and because I had not figured out he'd given me the wrong assignment, I tried to move the wrong train. He screamed at me, called me stupid, then told me, "I sincerely believe, Mr. Crane, you will not last another month on this job." He was so bizarrely aggressive I had a hard time taking him seriously.

Three years later, the same guy was transferred to work a tower on a subway line that I was a regular on. He absolutely cooed when he saw me. As if he were the angel twin of that other guy, he introduced himself to me sweetly. "Mr. Crane, I am new to this line, and I look forward to working with you," he said with an appealing smile and soft handshake. I answered with little response- waiting for the other shoe to drop. I was sure he was setting me up in some detestably sardonic way. I watched him every subsequent time I saw him, only after the passing weeks realizing he'd either had a brain transplant or he'd received a nice little prescription.

My buddy, his Assistant Dispatcher, told me what he was taking -but, ask your doctor.

Even now, a year later, I can't help but study his eyes as he approaches me, calls out my name with joy, and wishes me a "...great and safe workday!"

So, if we want to say, without a likelihood of scientific contradiction, that "love" is part of the spirit, and not, rather, a physical part of cognition, we'll have to separate out that feel-good part of it.

And empathy, too. About 30 years ago, Italian neurophysiologists discovered "mirror neurons" when they noticed subject macaque monkeys they were studying had neuronal firing patterns when manipulating an object that were identical to neuron activity when the monkeys were watching another person manipulate the object. Since then, wide networks of mirror neurons have been identified in a variety of animals, including humans, and even in birds. Mirror neurons allow us to turn observation into direct experience. Further than the implications for skill attainment, though, are the implications for empathy. Studies on people who are more empathetic have shown stronger activations in mirror systems related to both hand actions and emotions.[7]

...And we'll also have to chalk up to physical brain activity any sexual stuff, as thanks to some absolutely dismal, filmed experimentation from Tulane University's brain stimulation program in the 1950's,[8] we know a mere electrical charge to a particular point in the brain can bring out wanton lustfulness. (Not that any man who hasn't made love with his wife in a while can't give sufficient testimony to the obvious physical- rather than spiritual- nature of lust.)

---

[7] For source/more info, see: http://en.m.wikipedia.org/wiki/mirror_neuron

[8] Baumeister, A. A. (2000). The Tulane electrical brain stimulation program: A historical case study in medical ethics. Journal of the History of the Neurosciences, 9(3), 262-278.

This reveals lust to be an electrochemical brain function produced by physical states of the brain, which are brought on by a variety of factors that only with the help of chemical or surgical intervention we can hope to gain any control over. Casper's Aunt Hortense, then, cannot be expected to be lustful in ghost form even if she was so in life, because she's left those neurons and electrochemical states behind.

The logical cogitation over one's love is out, too, as neural processing is scientifically understood to be dependent upon and attributable to the physical integrity of the neuron. Neurons process every last bit of information that the central nervous system takes on- all of it: motor, sensory, and cognitive. These are electrical impulses that cause excitement from one to the next neuron through an electro-magnetic process, understood by science, but which would take a chapter just to explain how complicated the process is, involving sodium ions and potassium channels, axons and repolarization....

I'd be a liar if I made like I have a handle on it.

Magnetic resonance imaging can chart neural activity and we can, in essence, watch thoughts as they, in the form of electrical impulses, "pass" through our neurons. Not like a rodent running a course, the process is better compared to a set of dominoes falling over- ones that spring back up after reacting, let's say. The result is not on some rodent that we call a thought that has made the passage- nothing is going anywhere. From one neuron to the next, a state of electrical pulse or no electrical pulse is passed- pure information, just like a domino being up or down, only a state of being is passing, a state of being, that along with billions of other states of being, will be capable of amassing to very complicatedly different states of being that we call thought.

It is the channeling of this information that makes what we distinguish as thought, not the very simple information itself. And the channeling is run by the evolutionary development of the very physical neural network structure.

The outcome of these passed states are nothing, either, beyond being other states of being; so that a lover's words, spoken in your ear, go through your brain's zillionious neural domino-dropping exchanges and eventually (a second later) result in your mouth moving open, your vocal cords vibrating the air, your tongue whipping the vibrated air that will carry a pattern that your lover's brain will decode as "I love you, too,

Sweetheart," and new firing patterns stored away in memory neurons.

Particularly disturbing are filmed accounts of amnesia victims whose brains reset every couple minutes or so. They behave exactly the same over and over again, never varying their responses to conversation or visual stimulation. Like robots.

Neuroscientist, Antonio Damasio, tells us, "Consciousness begins as the feeling of what happens when we see or hear or touch."[9] His use of the word "feeling" is perhaps a romantic indulgence used in a failed attempt to try to improve upon what pioneering psychologist, William James, intuited quite perfectly 90 years before there was any such thing as an MRI: "Sensations, once experienced, modify the nervous organisms, so that copies of them arise again in the mind after the original outward stimulus is gone. No mental copy, however, can arise in the mind, of any kind of sensation which has never been directly excited from without."[10]

Putting aside the channeling of information, how about those memories? Just considering me having no memories of my lovely wife, I really can't see how I'd have any love for her. It just needs those neurons to be love. Yet, memories are no more spiritual than the stuff sitting on your kitchen shelves. They are neurons, of a type that are good at holding their firing patterns the same, to which certain types of information are routed, originally for the purpose of defense, but, at this stage in our evolution, for much more lofty purposes.

In the September, 2008 issue of the journal "Science," a variety of researchers published reports of their success in recording individual brain cells in the act of summoning a spontaneous memory.[11] The recordings were made through tiny electrodes implanted in patients' brains. The recordings demonstrated that the same individual neurons that are used for a specific memory's storage are re-fired for its retrieval. The recordings actually preceded the patient's recall by a moment, enabling researchers to know a memory was on its way before the patient knew.

---

[9] Damasio, Antonio, (1999) The Feeling of What Happens, p.26
[10] James, William (1890). *The Principles of Psychology. P.44.*
[11] For source/more info, see:
http://www.nytimes.com/2008/09/05/science/05brain.html?_r=2&partner=rssn yt&emc=rss&oref=slogin&oref=slogin

Memories, then, can't take flight with Casper, as they have at their base the weight and substance of the particular physical formulation of a particular neuron. And, even when he was a physical human being, Casper could not claim any integrity to his overall being or spirit- because our physical parts do not belong to us. They are connected through vulnerable physical attachments. A piece of a brain can be taken from a person by the whim of accident or disease.

So, the "Love" that I wish to glorify is made up of a variety of vulnerable physical states. And it is nothing hovering like an invisible glob in my body, but actual physical things in actual physical states of being.

So what's left now? Have I taken everything from love? What is left to make Casper love a person? He is in no way under the influence of a good mood, sexual attraction, empathy, lyrical cogitation, or in possession of any memories. Is there anything left we might call the spirit?

There *is* something left.

Natural selection has made us a moral species, in part, due to the advantages of reciprocal altruism. Selfish, friendless humans did not survive as well as those whose brains were better inclined toward community. We have developed such an impulsive empathy that primatologist, Frans de Waal, calls it an "automated response."[12] We can find a physically manifestation of it in our scleras, or the whites of our eyes, which are three times as large as any other primate because they help us to see what each other are looking at when working cooperatively. In Why We Cooperate, developmental psychologist, Michael Tomasello, shows how, from childhood, we are naturally inclined to help each other, without being trained or even encouraged to do so. [13]

We might place parental bonding and loving parental nurturance as the source of that impulsive cooperation. After all, it is well-documented how humans who have been shown to be neglected of loving nurturance as babies are severely developmentally retarded, even though they were provided all their other needs.[14]

---

[12] de Waal, F. (2009). The age of empathy. New York, NY: Crown.
[13] Tomasello, M. 2009. Why We Cooperate. MIT Press.
[14] Harry F. Harlow, "The Nature of Love" in American Psychologist, 13, 673-685

Our evolution necessitated that parental nurturance. Unlike other mammals, human babies are born so early in their development that they require nurturance for a particularly long period of time. Our babies are born early because their big-brained heads must emerge early enough in their development to allow them to fit through a birth canal that was narrowed by their mother's switch to bipedalism four million years ago-uprightness that allowed Mom to have a better perspective on the foods she might gather and on the threats that existed around her.[15]

A picture of our brain's true nature emerges that is both fascinating, familiar, and friendly to a person who takes an interest in science or in the way even our own human inventions work. None of it is spiritual.

As for the spirit, the only trait you might safely ascribe to it would need to be irrefutable by definition, such as by saying something like, "My spirit is the self-aware part of me." As proof, you might offer, "A rock does not have self-awareness."

That statement rings true not because rocks have no self-awareness or because we do have it, but because neither of those claims can be proved *wrong*.

But neither can be proven, either. I can prove you speak the words that you are self-aware, but I can't prove it's true. You are, in essence, telling me there's a little homunculus in you who you can witness to me you know they know that you are there. It's ridiculous.[16] And if you prefer to ascribe to belief in a homunculus, you have not proved self-awareness, as the avoided question simply becomes how can the homunculus testify to his own self-awareness.

Besides that, you are witness to a great many things that are pure drivel. Like when you dream about things that really, really seem like they are happening. You are not an objective judge of what you know.

I hear you: "Oh, come on!" you protest. "It is obvious we are self-aware." Or, on the flip side: "You can't seriously say a rock might be self-aware!"

---

[15] Betty McCollister, "The Social Necessity of Nurturance" in Humanist (January, 2001).
[16] For source/more info, see:
http://select.nytimes.com/gst/abstract.html?res=F60610FB3A5B0C758CDDA10894DD494D81&scp=2&sq="can%20of%20beets"&st=cse

But, a computer can think about itself, too. It can be programmed to even act out emotions. I say, "act out" because "feel" is only used with humans. The difference between "feel" and "act out" is the indefinable value that would help define what a "spirit" is.

How about a rock? Well, a computer is made up of all sorts of inorganic material found in the earth. We might as well call that a rock. But, to make the argument harder, let's just look at the rock.

A few years back, I decided to shake off the aversion to science I'd taken for granted since my first year at NYU when I dropped Chemistry 101 after finding the first 15 minutes of the first lecture unintelligible. Now, I started studying basic principles of science all over again before focusing in on the more difficult theories to get an elementary understanding of relativity, string theory, and quantum physics. I found science is not such a tough nut to crack if I can approach it from my own angles of inquiry and at my own pace.

One of the great openings of my eye: when food producers advertise "vitamins and minerals," they are referring to the same minerals you find in a geology book. Of course, it all seems obvious now, but I'd never connected the zinc, iron, and magnesium on the side panel of the Fruity Bran box to the zinc they make roof gutters with, the iron cast to be a fire hydrant, and the metal spun for the Corvette's "mag wheels." So there is stuff in the dirt we must eat on a regular basis or we'll quickly wither and die. Of course this is true. We evolved here on a planet covered with dirt, munching mainly dirty plants for our subsistence that appeared just out of the dirt and rain.

Another eye-opener: Science is confident that humans and plants are from the same lineage. We are both directly descended from the blue-green algae of 3.5 billion years ago.[17]

And then I stumbled on the Miller-Urey experiment,[18] where a couple of University of Chicago scientists were able to create organic material from inorganic material. By mixing up ammonia, water, methane and hydrogen in a closed system of glass jars in a process of evaporation, fog, and electric shocks,

---

[17] Broda, E. (1975) "The Evolution of Bioenergetic Processes". Pergamom Press, Oxford
[18] Miller, Stanley L. (May 1953). "Production of Amino Acids Under Possible Primitive Earth Conditions". Science 117: 528.

Our Evolution

4 elements

hydrogen	carbon
1	6
H	**C**
1.0079	12.011
nitrogen	oxygen
7	8
N	**O**
14.007	15.999

→

Amino Acids

CH₃

O

OH

NH₂ H

→

Proteins
(amino acids chained in genetic code)

PRIMATE!
(stereoscopic vision, oppositional thumbs, really big brains)

Algae
(photosynthesis)

Mammal
(4-chambered heart, hair, warm blood, mammary glands)

Sponge (motile)

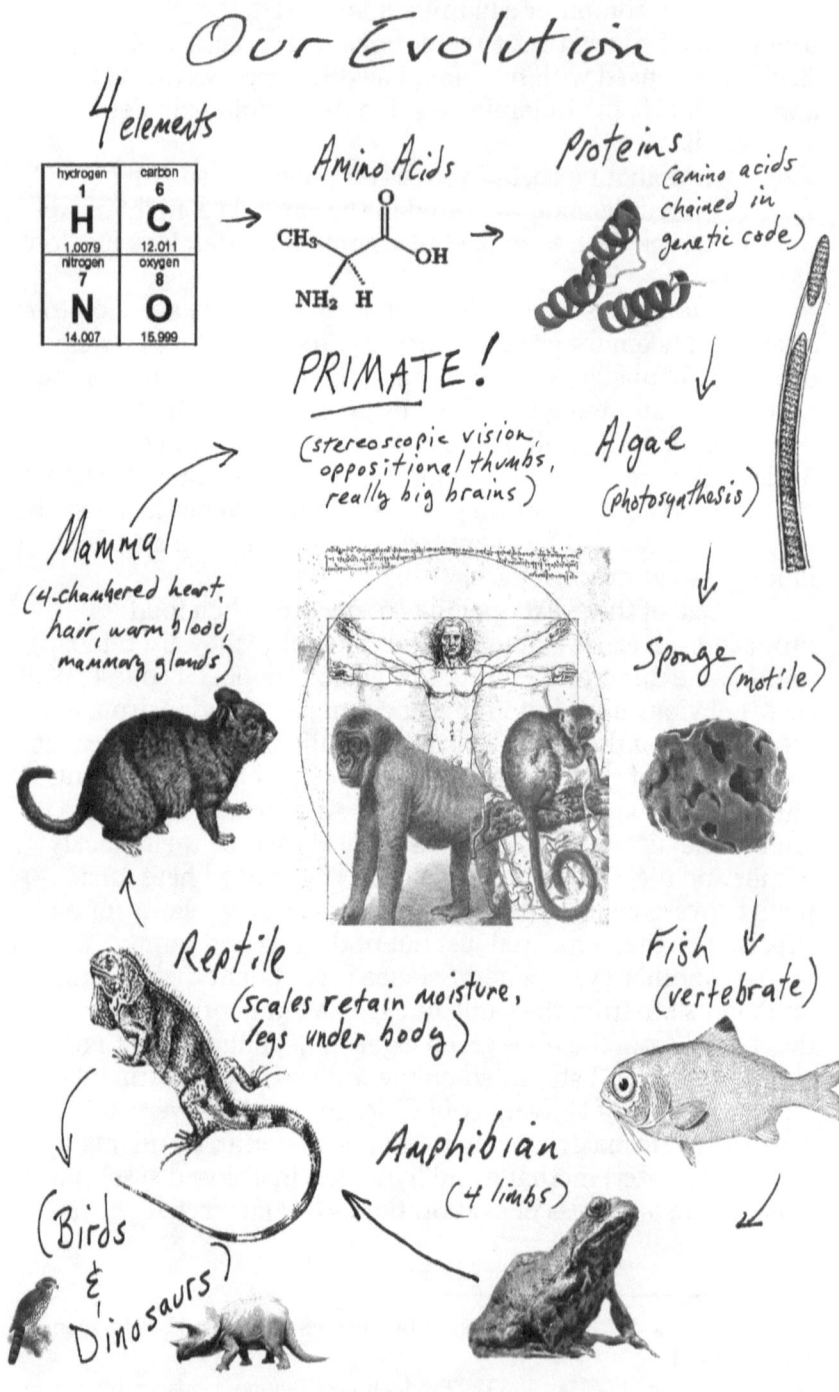

Reptile
(scales retain moisture, legs under body)

Fish
(vertebrate)

Amphibian
(4 limbs)

(Birds & Dinosaurs)

meant to recreate primordial conditions of rain and lightning here on Earth, they produced 22 amino acids- what are commonly referred to as the building blocks of life.

Once you understand the experiment, it leaves you with a confusion as to why it is really so important. Once you can see the continuum, the categories of organic and inorganic cease to have the magical boundaries that give the experiment its drama.

But a rock can't be self-aware. It can't even think!

Well, do you really need to think to have self-awareness? That is a question that cannot so easily be answered. If it is merely a process of the brain's physical thought processes to be self-aware, and that is the one definition we can place on the spirit, then the spirit is wholly bound in the confines of the organic human brain.

A rock might very well be self-aware if we posit that self-awareness exists in a different area, independent of the physical processes of the brain.

Just like the self-attesting nature of the assertion to being self-aware, the source of people's belief that they are more spiritual than rocks is often predicated on humans being somehow "higher" than other things. From birth, we are taught to see ourselves that way. We eat other mammals. We kill rodents and swat flies. Our roads go through mountains rather than over them. We are willful creatures, constantly affecting the world around us in directions we glorify.

There is nothing inherently glorious about a cathedral if first you haven't been given the notion that cutting and moving large blocks of rock is better than sitting there singing a song. There is nothing glorious about reflecting on the course of the stars across the sky if you are not a thinking creature. In fact, to a stupid mosquito there is nothing *less* glorious than the latest wonder of bug-zapper technology.

We can dominate and kill other animals, which makes us greater.

Well, even if you accept the notion that dominating and killing is more advanced than not doing so, such logic would elevate the world's most awful human specimens above its finest. Stalin over Gandhi.

We are emotional.

Yes, well that's what we are.

We are verbal.

These are not things that prove we have invisible, everlasting identities. These are simply descriptions of our physical differences from other forms. A human is not any higher than a monkey or a shred of blue-green algae. If being a human were so great, they would not need such a thing as a monkey cage to get monkeys to come along to the zoo. Birds can fly, but we can't. Bats, whales, and dolphins use sonar. Birds and bees can see a greater share of the electromagnetic spectrum than humans (who can detect a mere 1.5%.) The most complex structure in the known universe is the brain of the blue whale, compared to whose brain, ours is puny. Dogs smell better and hear better than us. We may be able to show a dog is *different* from a fish in that a dog can express sorrow at the loss of a loved one, but we cannot say the dog's emotional capacity as perceived by us makes the dog any *better*. There is no scientific or rational basis for the value.

We marvel at how perfect and complicated the design of the universe is,[19] another example of this narcissism, as the universe's design is only sophisticated relative to our ability to understand it, not by some universal standard of sophistication (which would, of course, rate the universe's design to be of average sophistication, by definition.)

Not that my idea of what a spirit is supposed to be is the bottom line. There are people- maybe you're one of them- who are inspired by a concept of spirit that includes even rocks and plants. There are those who see spirit as being separate from memories and something that carries forth without any ability by your memory to stay in residence. And that somehow still inspires their faith.

There are people who, perhaps inspired by string theory, believe everything is connected and interrelated. They call that spirituality.

But the farther away you get from the very material God of old Charlton Heston movies- however much you may become more rationally reasonable- you move farther from saying anything relevant or consequential to our daily struggles.

---

[19]http://flashcarddb.com/cardset/79150-re-believing-in-god-flashcards

Spirituality is all about finding answers, isn't it? It is about gauging meaning. Truth. Real truth, right?

The question then must be: In the face of scientific insights, where do we find the real truth that gives our lives meaning?

In its premise that threatens to measure faith with fact, this question offends religious orthodoxy, promising to repel those who abide comfortably in faithful convention. But, the truth is not encased in amber. It is not to be found scratched on some ancient cuneiform tablets, nor penned elaborately on some yellowed scroll of parchment. It is up ahead there. Keep your eyes peeled...

Victor, "Wild Boy of Aveyron"

Early in 1798, in the mountains of Southern France, a strange, filthy, naked boy, of about nine or ten, was captured by villagers who had found him running in the woods. He was covered with scars, he was indifferent to bitter cold weather, he understood no language, he was "unhousebroken," he was completely intolerant of clothing, and he would refuse virtually all food but water and root vegetables. He moved always at a trot or gallop, and he showed no ability to focus his attention. The sole human trait he displayed was an ability to stand upright.

After being put on public display, he escaped, but he was recaptured 2 years later near the village of Saint-Sernin.

His case drew the attention of the French public, and he soon became known as the "Wild Boy of Aveyron." From that point, the boy, who they named "Victor," was under the care of scientists, educators, and benefactors. Though Victor never learned to use spoken language, the doctor who trained Victor claimed Victor made significant progress from his initial state:

> *Such was the state of this boy's physical and moral faculties that he ranked not only among the lowest of his species but even among the lowest animals. One could go so far as to say*

*that he differed from a plant only because he
could move and make sounds.*[20]

And, as a man, despite much intervention, he only made a little more progress, still described as "half wild"[21] by an anthropologist shortly before Victor's death in 1828.

There are several well-documented historical cases of "feral children," who are left alone in formative stages of their early childhood. Though these cases vary depending on the extent they were nurtured and/or abused, a review of these cases makes it apparent that a child who is neglected loving human guidance will fail to develop many vital human traits, such as language, remorse, sorrow, anticipation of the future, an upright gait, artistic expression, selflessness, trust, knowledge and an ability to use it to improve... And, in fact, depending on how extreme, the child will have great trouble developing even rudimentary versions of these traits later in life despite much effort by scientists, social workers and educators to correct the damage.

Just about everything we are that we think of as distinguishing ourselves as human we get from observing, learning, patterning, modeling from some external guidance. This need for guidance is as integral a part of our humanity as our frontal lobe. Even the most critical and skeptical of us get everything we are from the sources we scrutinize. It is our only way of becoming human.

Go back 150,000 years, and humans with essentially the same cognitive capabilities as you or I functioned much like these feral children. It has been an evolution- not the physical type popularized by Darwin- but an evolution of nurturance and enculturation, instilling vital skills and understandings, as it has been passed down from one generation to the next over those thousands of years that has made us human. Today, as babies, we are unformed, no different than the babies of tuber-rooting humans who had yet to develop a proper language. Just a few years of loving nurturance brings us from that bestial state to our modern sophistication, over a hundred thousand years of progress.

---

[20] see Shattuck, Roger, *The Forbidden Experiment* (New York: Farrar, Straus, and Giroux, 1980) pp.160-161.
[21] see Shattuck, p. 177.

Focus, skillful movement, the control over our environment, empathy, cooperation, skills related to food, health, and hygiene... and so on. All these abilities develop in early childhood at a nurturing parent's guidance separating us from Victor of Aveyron, and together they are perhaps as vital to being human as our memories.

So, it is reasonable that our highest intellectual aspiration should be finding out the ultimate meaning, learning the reason, finding the end point, the great father/mother that guides us to finally end our insecurity for once and for all. Our life's main struggle, to grow and learn, the struggle that makes us human, must end somewhere to relieve our most basic anxiety- purpose.

What is it that religious people have that atheists do not? A place outside oneself to source one's own actuation, finding final release of responsibility, a great peace and settlement. A place of final belonging and security that is reached by finding a point at which knowledge stops expanding and finally ends. This ideal answers to the basic earthly needs of a creature that has evolved to master striving for security and belonging in the natural world. Heaven is a cognitive achievement.

And, so, too, humanity achieves nothing greater than its own earthly concepts in heaven. Belonging, survival, peace, settlement, and security are each human experiences. Their idealization does nothing to change them—it only makes them last longer or more constantly.

Seeking this ideal place is a reward-focused or needs-satisfying self-focused journey

A child, too young yet to have developed speech, crawls across the living room carpet, eyes focused on an extension cord, and from the other side of the room comes a voice: "Don't touch," introducing a stressor.

The subsequent intellectual industry of that child's life will ultimately lead to the source of that voice's authority over the child's will.

In the face of scientific insights, where do we find the real truth that gives our lives meaning?

This is not a question for any of us to fear.

Chapter Three
Poor Foundations for Faith

*God has good reason to give us faith, for there is someone
completely trustworthy for us to believe in and be saved by. The
faith he gives us is rooted in his Son, who became flesh for our
salvation. We have good reason to have faith, for we have a
Savior who has purchased our salvation for us. He has done all
that it takes, once for all, signed, sealed and being delivered.
Our faith has a firm foundation: Jesus Christ.*
– Pastor Joseph Tkach[22]

*Faith is simply surrender: I yield myself to the impression the
tidings I hear make on me. By faith I yield myself to the living
God. His glory and love fill my heart, and have the mastery
over my life. Faith is fellowship; I give myself up to the influence
of the friend who makes me a promise, and become linked to
him by it. And it is when we enter into this living fellowship
with God Himself, in a faith that always sees and hears Him,
that it becomes easy and natural to believe His promise as to
prayer. Faith in the promise is the fruit of faith in the promiser:
the prayer of faith is rooted in the life of faith. And in this way
the faith that prays effectually is indeed a gift of God.*
-Rev. Andrew Murray[23]

The word "faith" is often extended to worshippers in a
mysterious way. There is simply no complete way of
understanding it. "Faith" often comes up to explain the most
inexplicable of religious confusion.

The word "faith," though, is simply a word. Words cannot
be mysterious. They can refer to mysterious things, but the
reference will be particular and direct. If a word's *definition* is
mysterious, it becomes a sound. "Urgomp" is a sound. "Faith" is
a word. Words impart particular meanings. They can have more
than one meaning, but each particular definition must be firm. A
particular definition of "faith" cannot refer to different things at
different times, and a person who tries to use terms without
holding them to a precise definition is simply avoiding real
communication.

---

[22] "Discipleship 101" by Dr. Joseph Tkach,, WCG.org
[23] "With Christ" by Rev. Andrew Murray, CCEL.org

Faith does not refer to a large compounded mass of cotton candy that builds up in one's spirit after very intense bouts of prayer and reflection. Faith is not an unseeable cloud of heavenly smoke that leaks from below church pews, and, once breathed deeply into one's lungs, allows a person to set aside all reason to see the hidden truth in something very unreasonable. No. Faith is real.

"Faith" refers not simply to confidence, but to confidence in one's belief. You can't have "faith in God." You may have faith in your *idea that God exists*. You may *have confidence in* God. You can have faith in your belief that God will or will not do something, but you can't have "faith in God." The reason ministers so often impulsively lose their control over this term- they use "faith" as a synonym for "confidence" and drop off the part about that confidence referring to one's beliefs- is because their impulse is to becloud the nasty fact that people are actively choosing to adopt beliefs.

Imagine, one minister stands and booms, "We must have faith in our belief that God exists!" In the head of more than a few congregants, a question arises: *Do* I believe that God exists?

Another minister exhorts, "We must have confidence in God!" The congregant asks herself: *Is* God worthy of my confidence?

A third minister says, "We must *have faith in* God!" By misuse of the term "faith," the third minister has added a layer of confusion that can easily be mistaken for religious mystery, and simultaneously extinguishes the personal awareness of choice that sensibly arises in the congregant's thoughts. The end result is no concrete message, just an imperative for persons already disposed toward cooperation and fellowship to act without rationality.

Faith refers to confidence in one's beliefs. If enough people misuse it, it may eventually be listed in the dictionary as a direct synonym for confidence, in which case "faith in God" will be correct, but the meaning the preacher is seeking will remain the same confusion as before. When a preacher says to have "faith in God," they are not trying to encourage us to trust God. If you already believed in God, an omnipresent font of virtuosity, you would not need someone's encouragement to trust God, would you? No. He is trying to encourage you to lean on a *belief* in God uncritically so that a whole world of religious understanding can grow on a foundation you have not scrutinized.

The problem with that is that if the quality of the source of faith is not strong, one really doesn't believe a thing.

Religious figures commonly exhort their flock to have faith, and they disparage those of waning faith, but little attention seems to be paid to the source of faith.

What makes people believe strongly in their religion?

I offer three examples of common sources of faith in religious belief that I propose should be avoided for being deeply flawed:

The basis for that devotee's faith may be irrational. A lack of elementary knowledge can reveal religious devotion to be plain foolishness, such as in the case of the pamphlet-pushing lady I met on the subway who informed me, "Jesus spoke Old English," to explain why the Bible was so hard for most people to understand- or the talk radio show caller I once heard who said, "They dug up Adam and Eve's bones and did a DNA and found they were Africans!" According to a recent Pew survey, avowed atheists demonstrated a significantly greater knowledge of religious teachings, history, and leadership than those avowed to a particular religious belief,[24] which demonstrates how widely-spread may be this flawed source of faith. Mark Twain observed, "It ain't what you don't know that gets you into trouble. It's what you know for sure that just ain't so."

People sometimes get caught in a fetish of their own cultural group. Say you believe in God because you believe that anything said by your local pastor, your religion's greater leadership, or even the religiously-demagogic political leadership in your society is right and that it is just evil to question those authorities. Your abdication of control to the cultural group expunges your ability to claim or disclaim any responsibility for your behavior.

People often believe tradition validates religious belief. You may, like some, believe human thought to be so insignificant that you have a laconic disinterest in justifying your beliefs, even to yourself. You will just plod on as those before you have, with blinders beside your eyes and a smile on your lips, trusting in the past. It is magical thinking that God has created an environment for you where mere obedience to the most obvious authority-tradition- is all that you need to do to succeed. Some of the greatest horrors of history have come from such silliness. The

---

[24] For source/more info, see: http://pewforum.org/other-beliefs-and-practices/u-s-religious-knowledge-survey.aspx

Salem witchcraft trials spring to mind, or Christian Scientists who have stood by while their children died of curable illnesses. Still, I would argue the problem is more elemental than is demonstrated by such notorious examples. I would use a broader brush and say that, when it comes to our moral maturation, due to our respect for tradition, nearly all humanity seems to be impotently waiting for the past to push it forward.

The course of history shows us truth and selfless critical inquiry will always trump ignorance and pride in the end, regardless of one's commitment. Ignorance, by its nature, has a limited lifespan. Every ignorance in the world is destined to pass away some day (...which is not necessarily good news, as in a later chapter I will address the separate issue of whether the ignorance will pass away in time to keep us from destroying ourselves.)

Some would have us embrace ignorance, asserting religion is not beholden to rationality. That sounds good- kind of an escape clause from all reasoned debate. Still, it is Kool-Aid® poppycock. Those who take cover with such a notion are under the mistaken impression that their own spirituality could not find a way to survive in the light of reason.

Religion must be truthful. It must be real. It must be intensely relevant, connecting directly to us.

And this is just where faith comes in.

In their failure to be scientifically relevant, many religions turn to faith. In its best form, this "faith" is something more concrete than, say, suspension of disbelief. Here, we are instructed to reach inside for an awareness that we are already invested with. This "inner light" is what allows us to see the higher, ultimate truths, and it is what makes it unnecessary to feel our understanding of our spiritual place is threatened when we are called on to acknowledge scientific insight.

There is not enough talk of this "inner light," though. Religious leaders tend to spend more time assailing failures of faith in their followers than working to connect them to their "inner light." If these leaders really did believe in this inner source of truth, they might rather be spending all their time holding retreats, like a Seventies self-awareness movement, with leaders urging, "Reach inside, ye of little faith! Find that inner light that God gave you!"

I see a pastor now, casting arms over the congregation. "All these people are here because they know from inside that God is here. It isn't belief in this group or belief in the Bible as a historical document they depend on. They are here because of the faith that arises from what they feel within, which gives awareness of God's purpose!"

Provided the "inner light" this leader refers to impels the propagation of the faith, such a leader will not waste time in debate or castigating others for poor moral behavior. This leader will be a mere world wanderer, trying to help every person to get in touch with that awareness God has bestowed.

But I'm not sure most religious followers would feel comfortable being limited to an inner foundation for their faith.

Let's try an experiment. So as not to offend, let's imagine a religion. We'll call it "Zezuism," based on the teachings of Zezu, a 3rd Century BCE healer, who is claimed by his followers to be the real God. Let's try to strip away the ungrounded sources for faith from Zezuism- those weaknesses I mentioned earlier- not because these poor sources of faith are necessarily poor components of religion- but, just as an experiment to see what bedrock elements are left.

150 BCE relief depicting Zezu with winged sun disk.

Let us imagine someone discovers a text tomorrow that, let's say, can be authoritatively proven to have been carried by Zezu. Further, when cracked open for the first time in more than two thousand years, this text has Poseidon performing all the holy miracles Zezuism's teachings have ascribed to Zezu.

The illusion of historical relevancy serves as backbone of faith for a significant portion of religious followers. Historical relevancy, though, cannot be demonstrated. Religion is based on texts that come from spoken-word tales that were passed for decades or centuries. There simply is no historical evidence proving any of religion's spiritual claims.[25]

So, with Zezu's book, let's say we've removed an irrational basis for faith- an illusion of historical relevance.

---

[25] Using the New Testament as one example, see Bart Ehrman's 2007 work, The New Testament: A Historical Introduction to the Early Christian Writings, Oxford University Press, USA.

If we also remove the possibility for fetish of the social group from religion, we will take a step further into the core of faith. Let's imagine Zezuism, having lost credibility with the whole Poseidon debacle, finds its donations plummeting just as its investments take a sudden downturn with the economy. Short on funds, Zezuism sells off all its real estate and replaces its churches with internet chat rooms that are so anonymous they don't even allow you to go by a nickname, thereby incapacitating the group identity to an extent that fetish, or tribalism, could never rise above a whimper.

And then in a foolish "New Coke"-like move, Zezuism changes its name to FaithWorldUnited.com, destroying its claim to tradition.

What would be left to offer those who had previously just followed blindly in the rutted path before them, whose parents and grandparents had been pious Zezutians?

If you were of Zezutian heritage, why would you log-on to this new religion?

Curiosity?

What would you be curious to find?

If you take away the false impression of a rational base, the group identity, and the tradition from your religion, is your religion still your religion?

Those who would answer "It is not," need to ask those who would answer "It is," the following question:

What is left?

Ideas that are not exclusive to religious thought, perhaps. Awareness. That character I told you about who is roaming the world trying to help people get in touch with their "inner light" would certainly still be in business. Inspiration.

What we are left with is a religion guided really by nothing but our faith in an "inner light," something we know somehow all by ourselves, which allows us to see our way to truth.

Once again, scripture may guide it, but only after that inner awareness has indicated the scripture's relevance, so that the inner awareness- not the scripture- is the core source of that faith.

Chapter Four
The Intellectual Challenge of Hope

All right, then, I'll go to hell.
-Huckleberry Finn, when he decides not to give Jim up.

Might morality be something that is more organic, more essential to humanity than religion?

In the Bible it is claimed, "God is love,"[26] a crucial connection for a writing that seeks to establish the eminence of God to a people who are naturally inclined to understand the greatness of the loving ideal. And it is an argument that must be made, as the Bible's god is often vengeful, brutal, and even immoral (by any up-to-date standard of morality.)[27]

Might this be another one of those cases where religious language introduces confusion to create a false sense of mystery?

God is an involved, willful being who is better than us. Love is not a being at all, but some distinct other thing. Love can be a feeling ("How Deep Is Your Love;") Love can be an idea ("What the World Needs Now Is Love;") Love can be a verb, too ("Love to Love You, Baby.") God is none of those things.

And if we were to blur our eyes and accept the confused notion, "God is love," love would be God, so there would be no need for religion. The concept of a person known as God and all the related scriptures and religious practices would be an unnecessary focus to a loving person.

We are talking about words again. Love is Love. God is God.

To offer the benefit of the doubt, let's go with a more linguistically intelligible claim: God is perfectly successful in his aspiration to being loving.

How close to perfectly loving are you? Does the closer you get to being perfect get you closer to being as great as God?

Is it possible that others are better than you at being loving? Would that make them greater than you? And if it did, might that be more due to your dysfunctional sinfulness bringing

---

[26] 1 John 4:8.
[27] For source/more info, see:
http://www.infidels.org/library/modern/donald_morgan/atrocity.html

you below them rather than to their good acts? I mean, why are you sinful? Shouldn't you stop it right away?

Or maybe you are not sinful. Maybe you do not do things you think are bad.

I would hope not.

When I was a teenager, there was a wealthy restaurant owner who attended my church with his family, front pew and center without fail, 10:30 mass every Sunday morning. I thought there must not be a more reverent man in the whole parish, the way he carried himself. (He knelt very straight.) Then, just before graduating high school, I took a job at his restaurant. Turns out, he was a monster. He treated his staff- mostly poor kids who commuted 25 miles to Paoli, Pennsylvania from North Philly- like garbage, hollering and insulting, ordering them about like dogs. He did no work himself, and made every last one work well beyond midnight, though it was clear they were too young to be out of school.

At best, this character acknowledged his sins in the little oaken booth through a screen to a priest who had him say a few prayers to cleanse his soul.

Social constructivism, founded in the early 20th Century by educational psychologist, Lev Vygotsky, studies the way each of us puts together constructs that we safely follow through the trying experience of living. Constructs are those roles we are taught, those assumptions we are trained to make, those human ideas that we don't really see as human ideas because we are so used to living them. At times, our constructs desperately need correction.

The concept that the devout restaurant owner likely ascribed to- that he was incapable of becoming a person who does not sin- is an immoral construct, within which he is able to live a life that is moral, but only with reference to the construct.

Inherent sinfulness is a corrupt construct. We can be loving. We must be loving. (Or we need to seek professional help.)

But how loving can we be? Is there any possibility there may be a person somewhere on this Earth who always conducts themselves in a loving, selfless manner? Or is that just unthinkable?

If every person on Earth can aspire to being loving just the same as God- if God and humanity are both on their knees before the altar of Love- then there doesn't seem to be any point in worshipping God, no matter how loving he is.

And if God were not beholden to the rules of morality, where would our allegiance fall as good, moral people?

Let's say God appeared in the sky tomorrow, and he proclaimed: "I know how I've instructed all of you in the past, but you've really taken this morality stuff a bit too far. I never told you that you needed to protect children or outlaw slavery and such. And, hey, when I said to stone a non-virginal bride[28] or a person you find gathering sticks on the Sabbath,[29] I meant it!"

We would just have to change some concept. Maybe some of us would give up the concept of a single god, and figure this one's an evil one. Maybe we'd decide God is really almighty, but he is morally flawed. But one thing for sure: There would be at the very least a large group of us who would fight that new god to the death- even to eternal damnation.

And we could expect many- a large majority, in fact- to comply with the edicts of the immoral god.

I'll tell you what makes me think so:

In July, 1961, three months after the start of the trial of German Nazi war criminal, Adolf Eichmann, Yale University psychologist, Stanley Milgram began a series of experiments that graphically demonstrated the willingness of the vast majority of people to follow authority into wicked acts. The Milgram Experiment[30] has been reproduced many times- even recently- in many different ways, and always produces similar results.

In the original experiment, 40 individuals were told they were participating in a study of memory and learning. Participants were led to believe a second person they had already met was set up in the next room with electrical contacts attached to their body, and that controls on the desk before the participant would be delivering electric shocks to that other person- we'll call the other person the victim- if that victim answered memory questions incorrectly. The participants then listened as the questions were asked and were then answered incorrectly by the victim; and then a sober, lab-jacketed authority figure instructed the participants to turn a dial to administer electric shocks. Through the wall, the participants heard faked cries of pain while they turned the dial. This process was repeated, and the authority figure kept telling the participants to increase the

---

[28] *Deut. 22* Verses 13 to 21

[29] *Num. 15* Verses 32 to 35

[30] Milgram, Stanley (1963). "Behavioral Study of Obedience". Journal of Abnormal and Social Psychology 67: 371–378.

electrical voltage, 15 volts at a time. Eventually, in addition to cries of pain, the participants heard banging on the wall, screaming about a "heart condition," and eventually silence.

Public Announcement

WE WILL PAY YOU $4.00 FOR ONE HOUR OF YOUR TIME

Persons Needed for a Study of Memory

*We will pay five hundred New Haven men to help us complete a scientific study of memory and learning. The study is being done at Yale University.
*Each person who participates will be paid $4.00 (plus 50c carfare) for approximately 1 hour's time. We need you for only one hour, there are no further obligations. You may choose the time you would like to come (evenings, weekdays, or weekends).

*No special training, education, or experience is needed. We want:

Factory workers	Businessmen	Construction workers
City employees	Clerks	Salespeople
Laborers	Professional people	White-collar workers
Barbers	Telephone workers	Others

All persons must be between the ages of 20 and 50. High school and college students cannot be used.
*If you meet these qualifications, fill out the coupon below and mail it now to Professor Stanley Milgram, Department of Psychology, Yale University, New Haven. You will be notified later of the specific time and place of the study. We reserve the right to decline any application.
*You will be paid $4.00 (plus 50c carfare) as soon as you arrive at the laboratory.

TO:
PROF. STANLEY MILGRAM, DEPARTMENT OF PSYCHOLOGY, YALE UNIVERSITY, NEW HAVEN, CONN. I want to take part in this study of memory and learning. I am between the ages of 20 and 50. I will be paid $4.00 (plus 50c carfare) if I participate.

NAME (Please Print)........................

ADDRESS ....

TELEPHONE NO. .... Best time to call you ....

AGE........OCCUPATION.................... SEX......
CAN YOU COME:

WEEKDAYS .... EVENINGS ...... WEEKENDS.........

The session was ended after the participants reached the 450-volt mark on the "electro-shock" device (well beyond where it seemed to have killed the victim.) However, if a particular participant refused to go on, the authority figure would stop the process, but only after this authoritative succession of verbal prods (in this order) failed to dissuade the participant's objection:

"Please continue."
"The experiment requires that you continue."
"It is absolutely essential that you continue."
"You have no other choice, you must go on."

The results: 65 percent of the participants went all the way to the 450-volt mark. Only one of the 40 individuals stopped below 300 volts, in fact.

Two subsequent variations on the experiment were particularly interesting: one where electric shocks were actually administered to puppies, so there was no doubt the participants could tell the shocks were real,[31] and one where the shocks were delivered to an obvious computer avatar, so participants could tell the shocks weren't real.[32] Both variations returned similar results to the original Milgram experiment, demonstrating how consistent is the proportion of us who are able and unable to resist improper authority. Our individual pattern of response to authority dominates what we do, whether or not the situation involves a perceived moral crisis.

The Milgram experiment demonstrates what can be so scary about religious zeal: We become incapable of seeing the flaws in our impressions of the world...

... when we choose obedience to religious authority and neglect the responsibility to judge the morality of our religion;

... if our religious thought is stronger than our intuitive understanding of the loving ideal;

... or, if we piously believe in a God definition, which, by some magical correctness, we are relieved of our responsibility to judge.

The earliest expression of such magical thinking can be found in the concept of purity, a concept basic to religion's development. What was originally a protective mechanism against health risks, like bodily fluids, diseased corpses, or spoiled or risky food, (carnivores, in fact, are the only animals to express disgust, due to the particularly dangerous threat posed by ingesting rancid meat;) the concept of purity eventually developed into pure superstition or areas where it benefited religious authority as a means of control. People who sin can be impure. Acts can be impure. Competing religions and those who practice them can be impure. Your hand can be impure. Your food can be impure. Things you say can be impure. "Penis," "vagina," and "erection" are "dirty" words. To "pollute" the minds of young innocents can make them impure, and it can cause them to do impure, "dirty" things that cause them to be impure.

---

[31] Sheridan, C.L. and King, K.G. (1972) Obedience to authority with an authentic victim, Proceedings of the 80th Annual Convention of the American Psychological Association 7: 165-6.

[32] Slater M, Antley A, Davison A, et al. (2006). "A virtual reprise of the Stanley Milgram obedience experiments". *PLoS ONE* 1(1): e39.

Popular with some particularly zealous Evangelical Christians is an event they refer to as a "Purity Ball" or "Purity Wedding," where the father and the teenage daughter go out to an "extravagant" event where they dance and dine, and the father presents the daughter with a diamond ring that she will wear until she gets married and is only then initiated into a sexual life. Sometimes they sign a "covenant," where the father promises to "protect" the daughter's purity. This practice involves a father in his teenaged daughter's sexual life in a charade that can best be described as romantic mimicry.

Of course, considering how vital sexuality is to our existence, holding these religious beliefs up to rational scrutiny reveals that there is maybe no notion so illogical as one that claims sexuality is "impure." Further, the concept of purity- that there are things that are wholly good beyond the reach of scrutiny- is a primitive, unsophisticated one, as is true with most absolutist doctrines of thought. These are notions that can systematically protect large groups of stupid people, but notions that, inversely, corrupt our progress the more intelligent we become.

Religions provide reasons for turning away from the intellectual effort it takes to renew our constructions of reality, and it is just so easy for an intellectually lazy person to cop out through religion.

The worst result is that a person who is only tethered to morality through obedience (rather than through their own self-concept,) is, though relieved of a burden, bound to fail when the rules are incomplete or when some other impulse stronger than obedience rises from their needs or desires.

Poor faith is the weakness of modern religion, it is true, but not because people don't know how to wear blinders- that's not faith. Religion's weakness is its failure to believe in the power of the loving ideal- then, to remove the blinders, to face whatever may come, armed with nothing but the truth of Love.

In a campaign speech, I heard Barack Obama say, "Hope is believing, and then fighting for things."

Hope is not optimism, but the clear-eyed pursuit of ideals. It is intelligent. It wraps its arms around everything- the good and the bad, both what proves us right and what shows all our flaws- before it lifts its eyes again to the road ahead.

In a life purposed towards morally idealistic ends, hope's inspiration is love. Love- not a divine intermediation that leads us to love- needs to be the central inspiration of our moral life.

This is a foundational shift of morality away from being religiously inspired to an inspiration that is foundationally secular, a transition many religions have already made, for instance, in the ideals of eating, dress and grooming, lifestyle, art, and law. This correction of the focus of moral idealism does not void religion, and it does not intrude on the concept of spirituality. A monk, living alone in the desert, might call himself spiritual, but he can never fear becoming immoral, as morality necessarily involves contact with some other person. It is not an ethereal sensitivity, but very much engaged in one's relations with others.

Yet, redefining morality as a secular concern has the power to unify all religions and atheism, too.

No sweat.

Chapter Five
Morality Alfresco

*We have the Bill of Rights. What we need is a Bill of
Responsibilities.*
-Bill Maher

In Chapter Three, I used the expression, "inner light," to describe
some awareness it is theorized God has put inside you and me to
give us an independent awareness to base our faith on. The idea
that this inner light is the final and only proof of God's existence
was used by the Augustinian brothers at my Catholic high school
to back away from Socratic lines of discussion that were not
leading in a direction conducive to the propagation of our faith.

Rather than just swallowing that pill, though- and rather
than refusing it- I looked for my own truth in it. And, what better
a concept to find your own way with than one that says only you
hold the true awareness, right?

For me, the problem with the "inner light" concept is that
my own innate awareness does not extend to anything concrete,
such as a particular fact, image, or person, including God.

In junior high, my gang of kids met up with a born-again
Christian, a grown man who came up to us on the street and
handed us pamphlets and tried to "save" us all. We each bought
it, and we tried very hard to be "reborn." I remember the
concentrated effort to contact the God in my soul. A very
comparable experience was when I, in the sixth grade- after
having seen a dramatic performance by a performer on the
Johnny Carson Show the night before- tried to bend a spoon
using "astral mind power." A crowd gathered around me there in
the lunchroom. I could've been elected class president in those 15
minutes. The spoon would not bend, though. When it was time to
go on to 5th period, I was washed up.

I have learned-knowledge and I have feelings. Maybe if I
meditate, I'll find more feelings. If I meditate and take LSD,
maybe I'll have more feelings and even see visions. Maybe if I
meditate and take LSD and sit out on the desert or in a Native
American sweat lodge for a few hours, I'll become absolutely
possessed by a host of heavenly spirits.

I don't know.

What I do know that is basic and that I couldn't change if
I wanted to is my own impulsive morality. I can tell you what is

loving and what is not. This morality is, I believe, more integral to who I identify myself to be than even my memories.

I'll call this my soul.

Soul: the actuating cause of an individual life.

This is not an atheistic idea, that morality is something intrinsic to human living on Earth. And it's not an idea that argues against atheism, either. In this understanding, the default character for a properly nurtured and healthy human is morally sophisticated, inclined towards empathy as a result of influences attributable to (pick one:) Nature, God, or Mom and Dad's love.

Who'd of thunk it?

The religion I was raised with taught that we are stained with sin. That was the default- and only religion straightens us out through various technical religious compacts with God. In ways like this religions usurp our concept of control over our own morality.

This is not to say that through religion we are not attempting to serve a good purpose. Often, too scared to move in an unpopular direction, people need the moral way asserted by a leader or group- we sometimes need to be led, but in the opposite direction than the way subjects were led in the Milgram Experiment.

People everywhere are out of touch with morality. And even people who were loved and nurtured and hugged and kissed as children often end up living immoral, lazy lives, completely out of touch with an innate, loving ideal they are capable of referencing. Before morality comes the need to make money, to score success, to impress family, to live a life like my parent did, or like a pop star does, or like a television character lived to such success. Like life's autopilot, our secure constructs, when we fail to question or revise them, remove our morality from our life's equation.

This detachment of me from my morality can be seen in no small way as being due to the marginalization of morality to the religious sphere, a tired construct in its own right. Rarely in our society does any agent provide moral instruction outside a religious context- not school teachers, not supervisors at work, not even the parole officer for a violent offender does so for fear of stepping on the toes of religion.

Which reminds me of when I did just that.

When I was a probation officer in New York City's Brooklyn bureau, I was given great latitude. As long as I had my pre-sentence investigations in on time, my supervisors paid little attention to how I conducted my investigations. In addition to banally collecting the usual information about job opportunities and family stability, however, I would always try to get outside the pre-sentence investigation box.

"Why did you go out with these friends?"

"Didn't you know they were going to mug somebody??"

"Why didn't you see this as your big chance to be a hero?"

"You could've stepped over and saved the victim. Rather than helping to beat him down, you could've stepped in front of him and lifted your pipe against the other members of your gang in the victim's defense. -Then, you'd be a hero, rather than a punk in jail."

...As you might expect, most defendants were blindsided by such questions. Completely unprepared by their lawyers (who weren't allowed to be present,) they would sputter confused replies.

"Is it wrong to hurt another person?" I'd persist, low enough that none of my co-workers would hear over the cubicle walls.

"But if you really do believe it is wrong, why would you do it??"

Utter confusion.

"Is there some part of you that does not think hurting other people is wrong?"

He wants to be agreeable, but he knows he shouldn't agree. He says maybe he thinks it's right sometimes to hurt people.

Even though I filled my reports with astounding text like, "The defendant states, faced with the same instance, he would again threaten the victim with a knife," "The defendant states he did nothing wrong in employing children to sell drugs," and "The defendant is unwilling to pay from his own savings for restitution," no judge ever changed a plea agreement as a consequence -not because the court ignored me, but because the court is simply illiterate to the language of morality. It is no less than taboo in our society to undertake moral instruction outside of a religious context.

But moral instruction is not only necessary for penitents, children, and criminals. Professionals, too, need moral instruction, and just as urgently. The strongest example can be made with the teaching profession. Recently, the New York Times monitored a discussion entitled "Can Teachers Be Taught to Teach Better?"[33] While various administrators tried to argue that teachers could improve by adopting various concrete practices that can be learned in grad school, there was a stronger argument made that good teaching cannot be taught; you either have it or you don't.

I contributed this:

> *A good teacher is not only a true expert in their subject area but good at communicating with inner-city kids... and highly intelligent... and emotionally intuitive... and sincere.*
>
> *Though many teachers are kind, that does not stop them from being dull-witted. They may be intelligent, but selfish. They may be friendly, but foolish. Immensely knowledgeable, but easily exhausted.*
>
> *Teachers need to be experts, communicators, intelligent, intuitive, sincere, kind, clever, generous, friendly, and they need an abundance of energy and enthusiasm. Think about it. Turn one of these assets to its inverse and you have a fatal flaw in teaching. Just one. A stupid teacher is worthless to a school. A selfish person, a dishonest person, a person who is emotionally needy or frigid. People with flaws like these are all around us, thriving. Teaching is one of the only careers where the professional cannot lack in one area. It just won't work.*
>
> *Say their only problem is they need affection and are not selfless enough to keep from seeking it from students in exchange for, say, homework. Or say their only problem is their parents never pulled them away from the TV, so they don't really enjoy reading and writing...*
>
> *Good teaching requires you have it all. Everyone else is a hack, and really none of them should be teachers.*

---

[33]For source/more info, see:
http://learning.blogs.nytimes.com/2010/03/03/can-teachers-be-taught-to-teach-better/

All right.

I return to the Times' question: "Can Good Teaching Be Taught?" Well, go down those assets I listed off and you will find those that seemingly cannot be taught cannot be taught because they are moral attributes, and in our society we assume morality is beyond the pale of instruction or job training. But let's consider what would be the situation if it were not beyond the pale. Let's say we actually believed we could secularly instruct adult teachers on morality. Let's say we had actually developed pedagogy for morality along with that we have for the three R's over the past 150 years of public education, and these adults had been primed morally as schoolchildren. Not only would we not assume teachers lacking in moral assets are beyond instruction, but a whole pile of those who are lacking would not be lacking and our public education would be considerably better.

And now, we can let our minds wander to just about any other profession, and it is apparent that morality is a neglected area of potential positive human development throughout our society.

Can the different religions allow for the idea that morality is a natural human trait that develops regardless of religion- that its absence is an aberration, a problem, a disorder? ...That the failure of a person to reject an unloving act can be assumed to be evidence that something is dis-eased? Perhaps they were not lovingly nurtured. Maybe they have a mental disorder. Maybe they have just been poorly instructed how to identify the unloving nature of an act.

How we would respond to these realizations is uncertain.

Should schoolteachers be teaching morality?

Should parents be held accountable by courts for their failures to provide their children proper moral guidance? Or for failing to provide loving nurturance? Maybe they are away too much. How involved should our society be?

Should courts be free to alter legal stricture for the sake of a loving ideal? Should they be required to?

Should we choose to restrict the cultural expressions of film, radio, and TV to those which are good, educational, and/or productive, rather than restricting them, as the current profit-driven market does, to what is most compelling and difficult to turn the channel away from? Which of these is a more moral version of censorship?

There are myriad possibilities for introducing morality into our collective policies, and each threatens to be intrusive. Consider this Constitutional amendment:

BILL OF MORALITY

We hold our moral code to be self-evident, that we will:

Engender in ourselves a sincere, respectful, and loving interest in our children.
Be respectful and loving towards children, ourselves and each other.
Pursue fairness as an ideal in our society.
Practice kindness.
Be truthful.
Act in the best interests of future generations, and so work on improving our world and our relationships with others in it.
Provide for the welfare of those who are unable to provide for themselves (e.g. children, elderly, indigent, handicapped....)
Make an effort to leave past conflict behind.
Express gratitude and seek forgiveness.
Seek knowledge.
Live courageously.
Cultivate an appreciation of beauty and creative expression.
Respect our natural world and environment.
Annunciate and advocate our ideals to ourselves, our families, and our fellow world citizens.

We need such a statement of moral principals now more than ever. Our profligate unwillingness to stop squandering resources and even just to spare our attention and concern for the sake of future generations- our children- has led to a perfect storm of worldwide crises- economic, political, and environmental. By the time our morality grows strong enough to reverse our behavior, there may be too few resources left for us to be capable of realizing the ideals that love establishes.

Chapter Six
Lighting a Fire Under Love

[O]ffenses committed by juveniles under the age of 18 do not merit the death penalty. The practice of executing such offenders is a relic of the past and is inconsistent with evolving standards of decency in a civilized society.[34]
- US Supreme Court Justice John Paul Stevens.

If my soul has a real quality to it of any value to me it has something to do with my morality- it has something to do with love. This loving ideal, apparent from infancy,[35] is our greatest resource. It is relevant across nations, across cultures, and across religions. It does not seek to marginalize but to unify. We can choose to attend to the loving ideal, to follow it, and to imagine where it might lead in the future, so as to better guide ourselves now. It is all we need to turn the world around.

It is the universal ideal of humanity.

This is very good news.

And it does not take away one iota from the ability of a person who believes that the loving ideal- or some other internal awareness- informs them of a particular religious reality to also practice whatever rites or beliefs that awareness inspires. And it does not take away one iota from a person's claims to religiously inspired moral reclamation. It simply takes away religion's ability to claim exclusive dominion over the moral sphere.

Religious thought regularly gloms together the concepts of God-is-good and God-is-boss providing little discussion of what thread of logic connects the two. If God is worthy of being boss because he is so good, then he is no longer in control of his worthiness, and there becomes a requirement that God be good, creating the heresy that God is subject to a responsibility he has to his subjects. Also, goodness, something we can each practice, becomes godliness, and we become capable of comparing ourselves to God, another heresy.

If God's bossness, however, does not require of him that he be loving, there comes a need for some primitive concept like

---

[34]In re Stanford, 537 U.S. 968, 971, 123 S.Ct 472, 475 (2002), (Stevens, J., dissenting)
[35]Bloom, Paul. "The Moral Life of Babies." New York Times Sunday Magazine 9 May 2010

blind pursuit of authority or some counter-intuitive mind-game on the order of a mystery we are too puny to understand (but somehow we aren't too puny to intuit that it exists, is significant, and that we are too puny to understand it.)

These unsatisfying explanations of God's relationship to the loving ideal leave just one more alternative: that morality exists separate from religious belief, that spiritual transcendence is on some other plane entirely. Religion can inspire us to be moral, and morality might even direct us towards some spiritual insight, but we might just as well find moral inspiration from a secular source, and we might just as well be led by morality in a path that moves away from religion.

Morality's genesis in the individual rather than in the individual's relationship with God is consistent with the concept of free will that is necessary to many religions, as some basic moral awareness seems to be necessary prior to the willful adoption of a religious belief, religions that reject predestination acknowledging some source that informs one's judgment.

Leaving philosophical inadequacies behind, there are practical reasons to reclaim morality from religion. In appropriating the loving ideal from the individual through the dominance over morality, religion saps it of its power. We are encouraged to pray, and in other internal ways, to practice a love that reaches no place it hasn't always reached. To practice real awareness of the loving ideal is to act with hope. It is not to sit with clasped hands, pleading, "Oh please help the starving children in the Central African Republic." To rather pray for someone else to act (ie: God,) is to fail to have true faith in that ideal. It is not even to be in the game- no more than a child wandering around a room telling other children to pick up the toys.

Our religions keep our focus away from our shared moral development.[36] Over the course of history, we have, as a species, improved morally. Enormously. Still, by the standards of what we are capable of, progress has been interminable. How very much too slow we are to change.

It is to most modern people a simple observation that the violation of a child's innocence is the most horrific of crimes. Still, torturing or molesting children has not been such a big deal

---

[36] In fact, a basic premise of apocalyptic religions is that Earth must, by prophesy, eventually degrade to a state of sinfulness so beyond God's control that he will need to destroy it. I'll have more on this in chapter six.

until recently, when we wanted it to be. Though it is surely the most vile crime, it is not even mentioned in the Ten Commandments or in the Bible.

This is because maltreatment of children was not criminal back then. With moral blindness, the writers of scripture could postulate on all sorts of outrages of the neighbor-stealing-oxen variety. But they were often plain wrong, like when they decried the failure of a daughter who's been sold as a slave to sexually please her master;[37] and they just couldn't get perhaps the most basic of all moral concepts: that children must be protected.

I. THOU SHALT NOT ABUSE CHILDREN.

How slowly we slog along, taking about the first 48,000 years of human religious behavior to begin to formulate it is immoral to sacrifice other human beings to the sky.[38] Then, it took another 2,000 years until we decided religion should not be killing women for witchcraft and to correct a slew of other cruelty to humans that had been going on. It wasn't until 1944 that "genocide" became a significant-enough concern to us that we were moved to invent the word.[39] We still haven't found a way to abolish slavery, racism, hunger, torture, or the subjugation of women from the world, though we as a world people are easily capable of it.[40] Here in the US, it took 300 years to abolish slavery, then another 100 to deliver basic human rights to those we'd enslaved, and now it's been 40 years since the Voting Rights Act, and we've finally found our way to electing the first African American president, a man who was just the 3rd African American to ever be elected to the US Senate.

In the Department of Health, Education, and Welfare's 200 Years of Children study, our own government acknowledges, "During the early years of the Republic, children were little more than chattels of their families- often referred to not by gender but as 'it.'"[41]

37For source/more info, see:
http://www.landoverbaptist.org/news0401/answers.html
38 "Early Europeans Practiced Human Sacrifice". Livescience.com. 2007-06-11. Retrieved 2010-05-25.
39 Pinker, Steven, Better Angels of Our Nature: Why Violence Has Declined. (Penguin, 2011.)
40For source/more info, see: http://gvnet.com/humantrafficking/
41 US Dept Health, Education, and Welfare, 200 Years of Children, 1976, p.

Until about 1875,[42] it was common for US children to be taken by communities or sold by their parents into public workhouses, almshouses, as indentured servants or apprentices as recompense for their parents' debts. Communities claimed the hard work was for the children's own good.

Consider George Washington's 1789 wacky presidential reflections on the practice of child labor in Boston, referring to girls working at the looms of a sail manufactury: "They come to work at 8 o'clock in the morning and return at 7 in the evening. They are the daughters of decayed families [the lower class]... This is a work of public utility and private advantage."[43]

A Washingtonian ideal: a typical spinner in a 1908 Lancaster, SC cotton mill.

But, don't write off Washington's moral lapse to some concept that modern morality was out of his reach. Here, a contemporary of those times demonstrates the absurdity of child labor was not something impossible to understand back then: "All processes of turning cotton... are performed by machinery

65.

[42] US Dept Health, Education, and Welfare <u>200 Years of Children,</u> 1976, p. 230

[43] John C. Fitzpatrick, ed., The Diaries of George Washington, 1748-1799, IV (Boston, 1925), 37-38.

[that is] operated... only by children four to ten years old... But ...[it] calls us to pity those little creatures. There was a dull dejection in the countenance of all of them." – Josiah Quincy, 1801.[44]

Above: The midnight shift at an Indiana glassworks, 1908.
Below, following: Breaker boys at a South Pittston, P.A. coal mine, 1911.

[44] "Journey of Josiah Quincy through Southern Parts of New England, 1801," MHS Proceedings, 2nd Ser., IV (1887-1889), 124.

Industrialization and the end of adult slavery disrupted this model,[45] but child labor persisted as paid work. Despite the country's mid-19th century developments towards compulsory education, until the 1938 Fair Labor Standards Act, it was still legal to treat your children as tools of your trade, working them in factories, mills, and mines, (or, until the 1974 amendment, on farms,) like mules or machines.

Physical abuse, rape, and other sexual exploitation of children have only been much more recently addressed through the 1974 Child Abuse Prevention and Treatment Act. The Catholic Church, in a particularly well-focused example, is still actively coming to terms with its extensive role in this pernicious activity.

Even today, though children are protected by choice laws; they are "nonpersons" in the eyes of the law in terms of competence,[46] and it is a brand-new idea that children are

---

[45] US Dept Health, Education, and Welfare 200 Years of Children, 1976, p. 230

[46] 200 Years of Children, US Dept. Health, Education, and Welfare, 1976, p. 439

citizens to be protected, let alone that their innocence deserves sanctuary.

So, this leaves an impression of a loving ideal that has evolved slowly, tentatively, but, like biological evolution, capable of dramatic tipping points of great change, such as the last 200 years, which are a minute segment on the timeline of human development, but which have introduced dramatic changes in our universal moral development.

The moral evolution of St. Nicholas, from 1852 to today.

The prevalent moral values of the modern USA do not apply to our view of the past, or we would not be so averse to looking back on Thomas Jefferson as a rapist.[47] Jefferson's reputation is

---

[47] DNA studies indicate Thomas Jefferson was probably the father of the 6 children of Sally Hemings, an African American woman he held as a slave on his plantation, Monticello. Though modern historians often use the word "romance" when referring to Jefferson's relationship with Hemings, this is not supported by even the slightest shred of evidence, and, in fact, considering the prevalence of plantation-owner rape of enslaved subjects, "romance" is the most counterintuitive concept to assume. The use of the word "romance" serves fans of US historical mythology, and, it is not actively stricken by African Americans who would perhaps prefer to salvage any possible active rather than victimized roles in early US history.

For source/more info, see: http://www.monticello.org/site/plantation-and-slavery/thomas-jefferson-and-sally-hemings-brief-account

sterling, whereas, if we look at a modern rapist, say, Mike Tyson,[48] we find a public disgrace. Tyson falls under our rules. Which means that some time between then and now changes that were inconceivable to them became conceivable to us. (It wasn't that Jefferson wasn't caught. There was a wealth of gossip about him while he was alive. Slaveholding rapists were plenty common in those days, and life went on obliviously, without a single construction of even local law.)

Our morality has improved between Jefferson and Tyson, but, failing to monitor our shared moral improvement, we fail to revise our view of the past. In leaving the past as it was, we lessen the likelihood that the more inventive among us may make the leap to imagine the revisions our future will subject upon our present. In looking back, for instance, on the esteemed Greek and Roman philosophers as being slavers and child molesters, we might be more likely to use a moral judgment when considering the esteemed among us in the modern day (think: modern executives power lunching in leer jets while babies starve in hamlets appearing smaller than anthills far below them.) You can see that this different outlook is scornful of narcissism and pride. It makes glory very hard to come by.

One US citizen who found glory was not content to justify his morality with a backwards glance. Abraham Lincoln used a self-conceived moral standard that was provided to him by his own ingenious foresight. This enraged legions of his country folk and even led to his assassination, but Lincoln's decisions supported creation of a moral identity that guides this nation's citizens many generations later.

Like Lincoln, we can set our moral course without reference to current standards or to standards of morally decrepit eras gone by (think: ancient religious texts, the early philosophers, or the Founding Fathers.) I'll call this "creative morality." Creative morality dynamically seeks out a vision of the future, (rather than the past,) of morality, and gets there with all haste. It employs an imagination capable of looking back on our time from the future with a scornful eye.

---

[48] Boxer, Mike Tyson was convicted of Rape by an Indiana jury on February 10, 1992.

LINCOLN'S LAST WARNING.

" Now, if you don't come down, I'll cut the Tree *from under you.*"

The political cartoon above is from 1862; the cartoon on the following page is from just before his 1865 assassination. The lady tugging on the arm of the savagely-murderous Lincoln is "Columbia," eponym for the university and the District, symbol of the European interests established in the Americas.

Once you realize creative morality, the acts we classify as evil lose power; become a real bore, like any other work that is waiting to be done. They are seen as only variants on the ignorance, incompetence, and illness that is found everywhere in this age of dying tradition.

Looking back from the lens of a future that lives in harmony with our universal loving ideals, we might find that today's narcissistic disassociation from the rest of the world allows our citizens to ignore the demands of our morality and makes it possible that grown men and women feast contentedly while, a mere airline flight away, whole populations want for clean water and a few scraps a week; that militarized nations rain bombs on helpless civilians without responsibility to any international controls; and that Earth's ecosystem is actively being destroyed with our full awareness.

As for our culture, the US media corporate empire is nothing but a rabid dog set after the innocence of every child in this country, panting at the PG-13 door to expose them to prurience and violence and insipid claptrap at the earliest convenience (to the point that the cartoon, "Yogi Bear," has content that necessitates a PG rating.)

Our culture's sacred devil is censorship, to the outrageous absurdity that in June, 2011, the Supreme Court ruled to overturn a California law that fined purveyors of violent video games to children. The video games specified were one in which the child would be trying to shoot President Kennedy in the head and another where the child would be attempting to rape a mother and her daughters. Justice Scalia, writing for the large 7-to-2 majority opinion, asserted that the law would have violated the First Amendment protection of children, stating law had no right to "restrict the ideas to which children may be exposed." Scalia, a conservative devout Catholic, made the common mistake typical of lawyers and religious followers in believing morality is not imagined creatively, but instead conjured from the past. Rather than bringing up Constitutional or Biblical conformity, though, he evoked the 19th century practice of telling fairy tales, reasoning that, as our grandparents were raised on images of cruelty and gore, so it would be wrong to imagine more lofty morality in raising our own children by restricting their access to the absurdly violent video games produced by the country's 10-billion-dollar-a-year industry.

"Grimm's Fairy Tales, for example, are grim indeed," his primitive opinion states. "As her just deserts for trying to poison Snow White, the wicked queen is made to dance in red hot slippers..., Cinderella's evil stepsisters have their eyes pecked out by doves... And Hansel and Gretel (children!) kill their captor by baking her in an oven,"[49] ...extensive references to a primer infested with anti-Semitic filth for a generation that would end in the shame of its concentration camp gas chambers and crematorium ovens.

After having made the sharp moral advances forward of the past hundred years, our age is much less stable than it was when it began. The changes ahead of us may rock religion more than the past age did, if for once religious people will cut themselves free of authority, and will pursue ideals only they can imagine; and, at that point, discover that others have imagined the same ideals. Others everywhere.

And the ones who will caterwaul in panic will be those tethered to the stagnant and ever-groping, ignorant present.

---

[49] US Supreme Court decision "Brown, Governor of California, Et Al, v. Entertainment Merchants Association," Decided June 27, 2011.

58

cried, quite out of breath, "I will give you your life if you will stop fiddling." The good servant thereupon had compassion, and dismounting the ladder he hung his fiddle round his neck again. Then he stepped up to the Jew, who lay upon the ground panting for breath, and said, "You rascal, tell me, now, whence you got the money, or I will take my fiddle and begin again." "I stole it, I stole it!" cried the Jew; "but you have honestly earned it." Upon this the judge caused the Jew to be hung on the gallows as a thief, while the good servant went on his way, rejoicing in his happy escape.

19th Century racial profiling: A scan from my 1869 US volume of Grimm's Fairy Tales, "The Jew Among Thorns" is a story where a man is tortured to give up his gold by being forced to dance in thorns, and then falsely accused by the hero and wrongly executed by hanging, and the only justification is that he was identifiable as a Jew. The lesson of this story, kiddies, is that Jewish people can be assumed to be so inherently evil that righteous Christians should feel free to steal from them and kill them by any means of deceit or trickery.

"You stupid goose," said she, "the opening is big enough. See, I could even get in myself!" and she got up, and put her head into the oven. Then Grethel gave her a push, so that she fell right in, and then shutting the iron door she bolted it. Oh! how horribly she howled; but Grethel ran away, and left the ungodly witch to burn to ashes.

Now she ran to Hansel, and, opening his door, called out, "Hansel, we are saved; the old witch is dead!" So he sprang out, like a bird out of his cage when the door is opened; and they were so glad that they fell upon each other's neck, and kissed each other over and over again. And now as there was nothing to fear, they went into the witch's house, where in every corner were caskets full of pearls and precious stones. "These are better than pebbles," said Hansel, putting as many into his pocket as it would hold; while Grethel thought, "I will take some home too," and filled her apron full.

More grim Grimmery from the 19th century. The children from the land where these folk tales germinated would grow up to demonize millions before robbing them down to their gold dental fillings, poisoning them, and then incinerating their corpses in ovens, systematically, en masse.

Chapter Seven
Leaving Evil Behind Us

*In hard times people are dealing with serious conflict
and...they'll often see themselves as the good side against the
evil side. I mean, that of course means you can't negotiate a
conflict. It means your enemies aren't really quite human. You
don't have to deal with them; you can just try to destroy them.
And that makes conflict, pretty much, non-negotiable.*
*- Elaine Pagels, a professor of religion at Princeton University,
in discussion of the Book of Revelations.*[50]

My mother introduced me to the concept of heaven and hell
when I was still in diapers. There is this place in the sky called
heaven and this place in the ground called hell. There is a kind of
invisible stairway you climb up to heaven, whereas, to hell, you
kind of free fall.

---

[50] WNYC's Brian Lehrer Show, March 9, 2012.

In Catholic high school, my religious instruction was broadened to include the notion of free will. We each have a free will to choose purity or evil, and if we choose purity we get to walk up the stairway to heaven when we die. It is unchanging, a kind of permanent covenant God has made with humans.

Well, not permanent, because eventually this will all have a horrific, violent end. The world will become so evil that God will finally have to throw his hands up and destroy it all, taking all the pure ones up with him and damnng the evil ones to everlasting torture.

Nowhere does this concept acknowledge the universal moral creep up: the rejection of slavery, the liberation of women and children, the growing empathy for the other animals humans share their world with, and movements keyed to protect our natural environment.

Our ability to morally improve through an ideal selection of random possibilities that nature offers us- not just individually, but as a people- is entirely neglected by religion, as if religion is just unaware of this capacity for change. Religion views morality as beginning with a perfection in the creator of humankind, and thereafter fouled by the free-willed subjects he created; rather than, let's say, an evolutionary view of morality, as something that continues to improve, and the perfection being something rather aspirationally located in the fore of the process. In this framing, religion actually may be seen as an anti-moral force in our world, busying the moral industries of its subjects with tasks such as prayer and devotions when they should be more properly involved in actively driving these changes.

Consistently, the stairway-to-heaven concept leaves no hope for our Earth-bound society to become ideal or harmonious.

The goal of the concept is to get up the stairway, and, in turn, whether you like it or not, forever separated from the society of the Earth-living.

Getting up the stairway is a trick of pleasing religious stipulations, not necessarily those of the loving ideal. For instance, to some religious notions a mass murderer who sincerely recants at the end of his days can succeed to heavenly admittance leaving a whole world of suffering behind him at the bottom of the stairway. The stairway-to-heaven concept's world-view allows for religious wars, purposeful ignorance, the degradation of nature, among a whole slew of imprudent immorality -as the only essential morality, by this view, is that which relates directly to the stairway ascent.

A particularly well-articulated example of this moral flaw occurred just after the Nazi invasion of Poland, when, at a crucial time for the safety of the world's people, Pope Pius XII's encyclical called for an abandonment of secular concerns so to instead focus on spiritual contemplation.[51]

In fact, as an atheist, I, for one, believe this stairway-to-heaven concept- which is not, by the way, essential to religion- is a significant obstruction to our world's path to morality. The failure of religions, which dominate the customs of morality, to engage with our world- to actively take responsibility for what goes on down here to victims of "sinners"- is reprehensible.

According to the Food and Agriculture Organization of the United Nations, world hunger could be eradicated at a cost of only 30 billion dollars a year (whereas global military expenditures amount to about 1.5 trillion.)

If bombing of civilians is wrong, then STOP it. If it is wrong for babies to starve to death, then FEED them. Religions perpetuate poverty and war by creating a space where they can be mourned and regretted, rather than diligently rejected. There are efforts made by religious groups, but these are of the bottom-up variety, rarely organized by religious administration. Who organized Concert for Bangladesh? A pop star. Who organized We Are the World? A pop star. Who organized Live Aid? A pop star. Who develops and distributes vaccines to poor children all over the world? UNICEF. Who organized a worldwide tithing to pay for relief to the people of Somalia, Haiti, Eritrea, the Central African Republic, Madagascar, Zambia, Burundi, Angola...?? No one.

Who led rallies to oppose modern bombing campaigns that burned villages, slaughtered large swaths of civilians, and drove millions to flight?

Acknowledging the efforts of certain stalwartly morally righteous religious leaders like the Berrigan brothers and Martin Luther King, I still ask where the counter-actions of the vast majority of religious leaders were when the Holocaust (10.5 million civilians killed) was being perpetrated, while Vietnam (4 million civilians killed) was being carpet-bombed, when the Rwandan (800,000) or Bosnian (8,300) genocides were

---

[51] Cornwell, John, (1999) Hitler's Pope: The Secret Story of Pius XII, Penguin, p. 233.

occurring, or when we were raining missiles on the people of Iraq (civilian casualty figures vary widely, estimates beginning at about 66,000 civilians.)

The fact of the matter is each of these slaughters actually had a religious component in its perpetration.

From the 16th-century pontiff Paul IV's invention of the Jewish ghetto and the required yellow Jewish identity badge, to the "blood libel" claims falsely accusing Jews of sacrificial killings of Christian children spread by the Catholic press, Catholicism fanned the flames of anti-Semitism that bred Nazism. Then, Pope Pius XII, decreed by the first Vatican Council to be infallible, famously sat on his hands throughout World War II, never opposing Hitler and Mussolini, making pacts with the regimes that empowered each dictator—pacts that made it a moral duty for Catholics to obey the regimes[52]. He failed to lead huge swaths of the German and Italian electorate who were Catholic against the Nazis, and he never threatened murdering fascists with his power to excommunicate. In fact, he supported the leaders of the Catholic-Nazi Croatian genocide, where Catholic clergy perpetrated mass murders of Orthodox Christians and Jews; and he failed to take crucial actions late in the war that might have saved the Jews of Rome from the German Nazi murderers.[53]

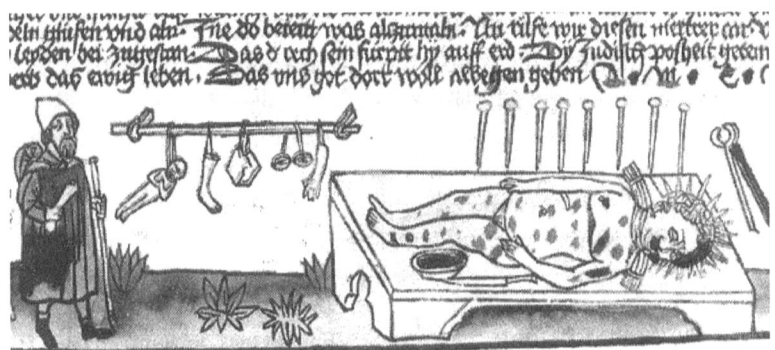

Simon of Trent, a boy Italian Catholics claimed was ritually murdered by Jews for his blood, as depicted in a c.1475 engraving. The church promoted blood libel by making a saint of the boy after Jews were tortured into confessing.

---

[52] Cornwell, p. 157.
[53] Cornwell, pp. 298-318.

Beyond World War II, one of the most prevalent cheerleaders of the US bombing of Vietnam was our country's most popular religious leader at the time, Billy Graham. Catholic priests have been convicted and sentenced by the international court prosecuting the perpetrators of the Rwandan genocide. A year after Rwanda, Christian language and symbolism were intentionally employed by leaders to encourage Christians to slaughter Muslim civilians during the Srebrenica massacres.

As for Iraq, the US invasion was supported vocally from evangelical Christian pulpits all over the United States.[54] In fact, the Bush administration seemed to believe they were on a new crusade against Islam. Just after September 11th, Bush said: "This is a new kind of -a new kind of evil. And we understand. And the American people are beginning to understand this Crusade- this war on terrorism- is going to take a while." Two weeks later, after he repeated the loaded term, "crusade," the press began publishing stories questioning whether Bush wasn't comparing US goals with the goals of past Christian "Crusades" in religious wars against the Muslims, and he was forced to retract.

Years later, GQ journalist Robert Draper revealed Bush administration internal briefings had featured biblical quotes (ie: "Open the gates that the righteous nation may enter, the nation that keeps faith,") and images that synched military and religious ideals.[55]

Bush's father had a similar run-in with charged phraseology when, during a speech to Congress on September 11, 1990, he urged a "new world order," a term raising fears on the left for its similarity to Hitler's "Neuordnung," the Nazi attempt at active cataclysmic apocalypse to bring about a Christianity-inspired[56] hierarchical millennium; and it raised fears on the

---

[54] Darrell Dow, "Pro-War Christians Should Come Clean," 12/8/2004 at http://www.antiwar.com/orig/dow.php?articleid=4127

[55] Draper, Robert. "And He Shall Be Judged (Donald Rumsfeld)". GQ (May, 2009)

[56] American portrayals of Nazism rarely focus on its Christian inspiration, many high school teachers falsely teaching Hitler was an atheist or pagan. He was raised Catholic, attending a monastery school that featured a swastika in its coat of arms. Though he did not attend mass regularly, one need only read Hitler's writings to know he promoted Christianity, whether or not it was for political ends. "My feelings as a Christian point me to my Lord and Savior as a fighter. It points me to the man who once in loneliness, surrounded by a few followers, recognized these Jews for what they were and summoned men to fight against them... How terrific was His fight for the world against the

right, for the term's historical use by statesmen, such as Woodrow Wilson and Winston Churchill, who some suspected to be the founding members of a power elite with an agenda for global domination.

Apocalypticism is a functional feature to many religions, the idea that evil will eventually dominate so much that God will be forced to destroy everything. The prophesy, though, is wholly dependent on the concept of evil.

What kind of world would we live in if religion stopped preparing for the millennium and, rather, began to enforce the loving ideal as if the millennium had already begun?[57] ...If the concept of evil was expunged?

In Chapter Two, I mentioned lust as being demonstrated by science to be a function of physical brain processes. We can draw from this that a person who is relentlessly frigid, or a person who hungers madly for sex every moment of their life might be, in a race of people of a similar physical makeup, quite normal. Their dysfunction is only a dysfunction in relation to the majority of their fellows who are unlike them. In this way, the "evil" residing in lust, one of the 7 Deadly Sins, evaporates. It does so the same way an awareness of depression may help explain sloth, an understanding of pituitary function may explain wrath, or that of hypothalamus disorder, gluttony.

This realization deserves no banner headline. We realize false concepts of evil on a pretty regular basis.

Just about everything to distinguish one from the majority has been seen as evil at some point in history to some culture. Skin tone, ethnicity, religious preference, sexual preference, marital arrangements, eating with a particular hand,

---

Jewish poison... it was for this that He had to shed His blood upon the Cross... as a Christian I have also a duty to my own people." [Baynes, The Speeches of Adolph Hitler, Vol. 1, pp.19-20, Oxford University Press, 1942.] Nazism, though, would not bend to religious authority. Had Pope Pius XII taken a stand against Nazism, who knows how Hitler would have responded. Regardless of Hitler's religious beliefs, Catholic and Protestant teachings preached anti-Semitism in Germany for centuries, which is largely why the German people responded with such zeal to the scapegoating of the Jews. See: c

[57] In their new book, The Last Myth, authors Matthew Barrett Gross and Mel Gillies present Apocalypticism as a terminal notion in that its riveting messages create an instability that makes it impossible to build level-headed, idealistic, trust-based constructs. We anticipate a moment of clarity, rather than pitch in to work on constructing it.

wearing or failing to wear particular garments, having a particular physical deformity, whispering, opposing authority, hairstyle, left-handedness....

A Midwestern woman, once confided to me- "You know, they're the kind of people who put mustard on their cheese sandwiches."

In Chapter Four, I argued that purity is a flawed concept, and here, I flip it over to assert evil- the opposite that is able to exist only fully dependent upon the notion of purity- is just as absurd.

I could offer how an understanding of cognition contradicts purity-evil dualism, recalling the unifying reality of the domino-dropping process of neural activity I described in Chapter Two, where thought flows through the audible vibrations in the air from one of us to the other, making us all, in effect, one (rather than dualistic.)

But, let's rather use our imagination. Imagine if people no longer believed in evil. Of course, there are unloving people, selfish or dishonest. There are people who do things that are horrific and cruel. But, imagine if we all start thinking of these things, rather than as evil, as quite normally a part of the natural possibilities- kind of like an earthquake.

Is an earthquake evil?

Religion would have you believe that to ignore the presence of purity/evil would be letting your guard down.

But, if there really was no such thing as evil, and we stopped believing there was, (just imagine the possibility, here,) the ground would be pulled out from under the stairway-to-heaven concept. Heaven's purity is appealing only measured against Earth's or hell's evils.

Understanding this, it becomes apparent that evil is as much a part of the modern God concept as purity.

This isn't just philosophical blather. It works this way on a practical level. For an example, I will daringly take perhaps the most divisive of social policy issues- abortion- and I will demonstrate the healing effects of cleansing the abortion debate of the concept of evil. The notion of evil is unnecessary to the debate, but to enforce religion's place or role. Once the dynamic of purity/evil dualism is removed, religion loses all significance.

I hold a Petri dish up. I poke a felt pen tip against it and now there is a dot about 300 times as big as a zygote. A zygote is a fertilized egg that has yet to cleave.

If I were to take the tip of my finger and swipe up the zygote, and then rub my thumb and finger together, some would say I am a murderer. I, like a woman popping a morning-after pill, have ended a potential human life.

Then, we'll move forward nine weeks to consider a brand-new fetus, (about the size of a bottle cap, looking a bit like a small shrimp,) not yet anywhere near the point it will be viable outside the mother. When abortionists kill such a fetus, it is the killing of a growing life that certainly has no thoughts as we conceive of them- as the fetus has no input source for intelligence, no concept of language, no memories related to sight, and no ability to feel pain.[58]

Step up to a six-month-old fetus, who is about 10-inches from head to foot. This fetus is much like the last fetus in their lack of what we think of when we use the word, "thought," but this one may be looking forward to sounds or to expectations of the mother's movement/sleeping cycle. This fetus is more aware, perhaps, of their own body, and, one very important distinction: this fetus has just become old enough that our society's science might be able to keep the child alive outside of the mother's womb.

Next, we have a newborn baby. Those who have nurtured a newborn know they are very much ill-developed, with no intellect, and just plain overwhelmed by neediness. Though mature dogs exercise a vastly more advanced intellect than a newborn human infant, human newborns are so dear to us that the vast majority of us in this morally-advanced age (as opposed to not-so-long-past other ages,) would categorize the willful killing of a newborn as murder.

Then, we'll consider a couple of years later, when they are developing rapidly as they learn to connect language willfully with their world, so rapidly that parents forget the unintelligent, needy lives these children lived when they first appeared as newborns. Even though, relative to human development, it is a new concept, it is fairly universal in our age that a two-year old's life is given equal value by world societies to a grown human's.

The killing of any of these lives would be regrettable. Some would seek to equate them all as murder. Fanatically, they

---

[58]For source/more info, see:
http://www.nytimes.com/aponline/2010/06/25/health/AP-EU-Britain-Abortion.html?_r=1&hp

may even seek to kill abortionists in what they consider to be a valiant act of defense.

And you and I might certainly argue about abortion. I would say any life that has not yet approached viability is not society's concern. Every life after that should be protected by society unless the mother's life is at stake.

That is me.

Maybe we disagree.

But we can't put this issue to a vote and go by a majority opinion without still having people barricading the entrances to abortion clinics and such. There are some extremists who cannot go along with the majority.

I would assert, though, that there is little difference between an abortion extremist and myself. Well, I'm clearly not referring to the murderers of doctors- I am not violent. But, as for the less wacko elements, I share much the same values.

We both believe it is not a good thing for a living creature to be killed. Even with a zygote, I would not argue with their conviction that it is a bad thing for the zygote to die.

I could live alongside this person and we might never argue about a thing.

The difference arises not from what is right and wrong, but from what is pure and what is evil.

I would hold that a woman who murders her 2-year-old child is a different person than a 16-year-old who, in shame, throws her newborn in a dumpster, who is a different person from a woman who decides to abort her late-term child because she suffers from depression and knows she will hate the child, who is different from a woman who takes a morning-after pill because she had a meaningless sexual fling.

Each act of ending any life is regrettable, and for most of them we can agree we need to engage a societal framework to help prevent them. But it is only when we employ the concept of evil that these issues get beyond our control.

To me, the mother who murders her 2-year-old is nuts, as is the 16-year-old with the newborn in the dumpster, but these acts are different and pose different threats in different ways to society.

To an extremist, all the aforementioned acts, from the killing of a 2-year-old to the morning-after pill popping, are simply murder.

Remove the evil, though, for a moment- the condemnation, the scorn, (save those judgments for the afterlife, if you will) ...and you are left with a variety of very different challenges. Of these challenges, we might all agree on methods to avoid future occurrences or methods to treat the more disturbed people involved.

We can argue about at just which point we need to try to step in between a woman and an abortionist, but we cannot argue whether or not their plans are "murder."

We can argue about whether a person who kills a 2-year-old can be rehabilitated by penal punishment or psychiatry, or whether programs to educate young girls about sex can cut down on unwanted pregnancies, but we cannot argue about whether a devil, invisible to any scientific methods of detection, is living in the heart of a person.

It is the concept of evil that converts a problem that we very well can approach and hope to solve as a society into a Maginot line, manned by those among us who are most comfortable with expressing hatred. The concept of purity/evil is an attempt to override our own independent judgment for the sake of a conformity meant to increase our security.

We do not need to be so secure.

When we change our concept of something from horrendously hurtful and wrong to "evil," we are pretending suddenly to understand it, we are making it unimportant, as it is already solved. We disown all responsibility for it.

How comforting to us. How easy.

We must find a way to stop abortions, but we can't do that by simplifying the reality. We need to focus on the issue, appreciate the different situations, and write laws and create social programs detailed enough to address the complicated realities.

Evil is a stigma to use to separate oneself from others and a shelter for frightened people to assemble huddled under. It is not a helpful concept to heal the world we live in here on Earth.

Just glance back through history. Try to imagine the German soldiers who dropped the Zyklon B pellets into the gas chambers doing so without being able to tell themselves the Jews were evil. Just try to imagine the Rwandan murderers finding some other reason to walk down the aisles of grade schools hacking off the heads of children with machetes. Evil is a self-perpetuating concept.

The idea that there is no such thing as evil is taboo in the US. The famous Pastor Rick Warren used the power of that taboo to push around Barack Obama in 2007. Check out this exchange between the carefully treading future president and the religious leader who clearly knows the central nature this question plays in the fate of his vocation in an intellectually developing world:

> Warren: Does evil exist? And if it does do we ignore it, do we negotiate with it, do we contain it or do we defeat it?

> Obama: Evil does exist. I mean, I think we see evil all the time. We see evil in Darfur. We see evil, sadly, on the streets of our cities. We see evil in parents who viciously abuse their children. And I think it has to be confronted. It has to be confronted squarely.
> And one of the things that I strongly believe is that, you know, we are not going to, as individuals, be able to erase evil from the world; that is God's task. But we can be soldiers in that process, and we can confront it when we see it.
> Now, the one thing that I think is very important is for us to have some humility in how we approach the issue of confronting evil because, you know, a lot of evil has been perpetrated based on the claim that we were trying to confront evil.

> Warren: In the name of good?

> Obama: In the name of good. And I think, you know, one thing that's very important is having some humility in recognizing that, you know, just because we think our intentions are good doesn't always mean that we're going to be doing good.

However weakly, Obama did push back by questioning our ability to define evil and good- a haziness that kind of contradicts the whole concept of dualism.

I would challenge any person who is knowledgeable in the fields of psychiatry and psychology to find one example of a cruel person for whom it can be proven beyond doubt suffered no abuse or head injury, brain-centered birth defect, or childhood trauma or severe neglect. As Investigative Probation Officer, I interviewed hundreds of offenders, and, it being my job to figure out why they were criminals, attempted to understand the reasons for their deviance. There was not one case where evil was a logical cause.

It was not that I did not want to believe in a supernatural concept like evil. When I was a kid, I fantasized about Bigfoot and UFO's and ghosts and the Loch Ness Monster. I would love to find a mysterious other dimension to life. If I could find the slightest sensible clue of paranormality, I'd be the head priest of a new church dedicated to understanding it.

But there just was no evil. There was a huge group of very-poorly parented young guys who grew up in neighborhoods where there was nothing to do but hang out on the street corners and sell drugs. Any day of the week, you can walk down to Criminal Court and watch them streaming through the doors in a current, along with all the wealthy judges, lawyers, and other law professionals who make their living off the industry of arresting and incarcerating them. These criminals may have long rap sheets, but every offense is drug-related. They are not violent at all. Usually, they are quite friendly, engaging, and respectful. Just like any other salesman. I would say they were about 85% of the arrests that came through our office.

Then, there was a smaller group of criminals who I'd call "bums." These men would commit just about any petty crime as long as it was not personal. They might have 35 arrests for breaking into cars, selling drugs, or shoplifting, but they would not have one single act of robbery or assault. These guys have no self-esteem, they are usually quite dim-witted, drug-addicted, and poorly connected socially to friends and family.

Another group I'd call "thieves." These types are shifty, completely self-absorbed, and absolutely untrustworthy. They are not violent, though. They are as evil as a larcenous act can make you. Of course, there is a difference between our concept of larcenous evil and evil that involves violence. Property is a human construct. One's personal security is not. It is quite real.

Then there was a group of men whose rap sheets focused, usually exclusively, on crimes involving violence or sex. These criminals were what most people would label "evil." Being severely beaten or molested as a child and suffering head injuries was very common to this group.

I discovered the histories through an interview, the setting of which was such that there was no advantage to the defendant in lying to me, as the plea agreement was already set. In fact, it was more likely a guy who would have rather not revisited his past would lie about not having been abused, as my questions were personally intrusive and not what the defendant expected.

Research has soundly demonstrated the association between childhood victimization and adult criminal and antisocial behavior.[59]

I read a great book around this time, <u>Base Instincts: What Makes Killers Kill?</u> , by Jonathan H. Pincus, M.D. The author held that a certain cocktail is mixed up in the minds of people we'd see as evil; a combination of neurological damage, psychiatric illness (both which damage the mind's capacity to stop violent urges.) and childhood victimization (which produces enormous anger.) A supplementary disinhibiting factor is the abuse of alcohol and drugs, involved in an estimated 70 percent of violent crimes.

So, I would come to look at murderers' heads for scars or dents as they were led into the interview cell. "Did you hurt your head there?"

"Ump. Yeah, that's juss somp'n from when I was a kid."

Or: "Did you get hit when you were a kid?"

"Well. I guess. In Jamaica things was different than you see here. Say I don't go to school- my Moms would tie me to the macoe tree and whip me."

"Whip you."

"Ya."

---

[59]Farrington, D. P. (1989). Early predictors of adolescent aggression and adult violence. Violence & Victims, 4, 79-100;

Farrington, D. P., & West, D. J. (1993); Criminal, penal, and life histories of chronic offenders: Risk and protective factors and early identification. Criminal Behavior & Mental Health, 3, 492-523;

Briere, J.N & Elliott, D.M. (1994). Immediate and long-term impacts of child sexual abuse. Future of Children, 4(2), 54-69;

Nagin, D. S., Pogarsky, G.,& Farrington, D. P. (1997). Adolescent mothers and the criminal behavior of their children. Law & Society Review, 31, 127-162;

Weeks, R., & Widom, C. S. (1998). Self-reports of early childhood victimization among incarcerated adult male felons. Journal of Interpersonal Violence, 13, 346-361;

Haapasalo, J., & Pokela, E. (1999). Child-rearing and child abuse antecedents of criminality. Aggression and Violent Behavior, 4, 107-127;

Pogarsky, G., Lizotte, A. J., & Thornberry, T. P. (2003). The delinquency of children born to young mothers: Results from the Rochester Youth Development Study. Criminology, 41.

"With what?"

"A stick is what. Whip me good."

It may be true that childhood abuse or trauma does not always or even usually lead to deviant adult behavior, but it may just as well be true that it is the main cause of it. To say I was beaten as a child, and I turned out all right, is a little like saying I smoked cigarettes and I never got lung cancer, (which doesn't go one step to disproving smoking is the leading cause of lung cancer.)

Evil does not explain anything with these violent criminals. It is not even slightly useful as a concept.

"Although sex offenders may commit other types of offenses, other types of offenders rarely commit sex offenses." - Center for Sex Offender Management, Office of Justice Programs (OJP), U.S. Department of Justice.[60]

If evil is a universal, why don't, say, shoplifters, dabble in child molestation? Why don't wife-beaters dabble in shoplifting? It is the nature of the immorality, not the criminal's weakness to the supposed allure of evil that decides if a person will be able to resist offending.

People are not tempted by evil, but by particular abhorrent behaviors that can be categorized.

And they are not tempted, but rather they struggle between parts of their minds that reason the acts are improper and parts of their minds that feel a contrasting urge or that reason in contrasting manners. Or, we might say, they are tempted by or struggling with themselves.

So, it is something that is organically a part of themselves that is the cause of the problem. An inclination to abhorrent acts is, in my book, already too far out of control for comfort. If I were tempted to do something I believed to be wrong, I wouldn't struggle to control it. I'd go have my head examined.

You may have seen the brilliant documentary film, "Deliver Us from Evil," where a Catholic priest who molests children is interviewed. He is not a frightening presence. He's just a creepy, puny little guy. He understands the horrific crimes he has committed are wrong. He regrets them. Really he does. He will even try very hard not to reoffend. But it is clear to the viewer that this man will never be able to resist the impulse to molest a child. The concept of evil would instruct us to, perhaps, send him on retreat and coach him to battle evil much more

---

[60]For source/more info, see: http://www.csom.org/pubs/recidsexof.html

fiercely, then reintroduce him to temptation- maybe transfer him to another parish- and ask him how resistant he's feeling.

Yeah, but that's absurd.

Knowing what we know about molestation, we should set the guy in a colony of his kind for life or until we find an effective scientific strategy to stop such urges ...as studies have tracked child molester recidivism at as much as 42%, and just avoiding one repeat offense is worth isolating a bunch of offenders for life.[61]

Punishment is entirely off-the-point. Punishment may make sense for something like insider trading, which is committed by people who know full well they are breaking the law, have the ability to act lawfully, but decide not to after rationally weighing their options, a rationalization that can be assumed to take into account their estimation of possible punishment. Punishment does not make sense when a criminal has no control over what they do, and there is not a stitch of evidence that people who molest children or commit violent crimes are failing to exercise an accessible control over their urges.

Here, where Evil seems most pure, it is most vaporous.

Frauds and cheats, however, seem to have more control over their choices. They may even have rationalized their immorality. We are creatures designed to hunt and gather, not to respect the concept of laws and private property, what are brand-new concepts in just the last tenth of the last one percent of our evolution.

Anyone who has had a young child knows there is a point in their development where you need to teach them NOT to grab things that do not belong to them; NOT to poke other people's eyeballs; NOT to push things out the window; NOT to throw breakable things on the floor as if they are made of rubber; NOT to punch or scratch other kids; NOT to swing large pieces of wood at other children's heads; NOT to scream, "I HATE YOU!" or "YOU'RE AN IDIOT!" or "SHUT UP!"

Children must learn not to do these things, not because they need to keep their internal evil side in check, but because bad things- things that we do not like- can be caused by us, and we must be nurtured to control our behavior appropriately.

---

[61]For source/more info, see: http://www.ncbi.nlm.nih.gov/pubmed/8370860 Hanson RK, Steffy RA, Gauthier R (August 1993). "Long-term recidivism of child molesters". Journal of Consulting and Clinical Psychology 61 (4): 646–52.

Since what we see as "bad" is not universally "bad," but "bad" only in terms of our societal constructs with others (remember the monk living alone in the desert who finds immorality impossible,) morality requires instruction, whether you believe in evil or not. Children must be lovingly and socially nurtured, and they must be taught to have idealistic intentions. It is no easy chore raising kids well.

And, as well as poor nurturance, peculiarities of the mind will also produce poor moral development. Such cases are not a testament to evil, but to our natural lack of control over our world, something that since the days of deadly plagues and civilization-leveling volcanoes religion has comfortingly assured us it has the power to secure us from, eventually, through escape to the afterlife.

Which brings me back to the child-molester priest: The Church failed to take effective action to stop him from reoffending, not just once, but over and over again. As a result, this priest deeply hurt many children. There was no religious wrongdoing, though, in his superiors transferring him away from prosecutions and to new victims, as the man's redemption was more vital a concept for the Church to defend than the ideal of Love, which would have rather defended the children's emotional and physical well-being. God can let children be victimized and mysteriously make up for it later in heaven.

Concepts that support religious administration, like evil, purity, sin, and redemption, are often in conflict with the supreme authority of the universal human moral ideal of Love. They work against our ability to achieve a better society, to evolve morally as a species.

The good news, though, is that, however much these concepts may slow human moral evolution, they can never stop its advance.

Chapter Eight
One World Tribe

So, I think to realize when we look at other people- you know, when we talk about other people, we say, "Oh, the trouble with him is..." or "She always does this."
Each person is a huge mystery. I am a mystery to myself. I don't know about you. But, I'm constantly surprising myself, wondering why I behave in this way ...
We know so little about one another and so that means we should approach each person as a sacred mystery- not thinking that we can sum them up or use them for our own ends or thinking that we know all about them and that's that.
-Historian, Karen Armstrong.[62]

The Pickering

On the 20th of August, 1800, the barque sailing ship, Pickering, sailed from New South Wales for Singapore, but was never heard from again. She was lost in the South China Sea with all hands in a gale that September. All the 118 aboard were presumed lost at sea.

48 years later, the British Navy discovered the then-uncharted South Seas island now known as Puhni. Puhni was

---

[62] From the 1/11/2011 episode of "Radio West," a talk show of University of Utah radio station KUER, Salt Lake City.
http://www.publicbroadcasting.net/kuer/.jukebox?action=viewPodcast&podcastId=228

found to be inhabited solely by descendants of the Pickering wreck. Bereft of shipbuilding materials, the survivors had been incapable of finding a way off the island, but they worked to recreate the civilization they'd lost as best as they could, making tree houses out of stems and leaves, fastening plumbing from bamboo pipes, and forming cooking utensils from gourds and stones. They had even a library, which was stocked with books survivors recreated from memory, the paper made from chewed malga root and the ink from fish blood.

The sensational news spread around the world, and fantastical stories were imagined, spawning the first set of "Swiss Family Robinson" tales.

Focusing mostly on the Robinsons, who were European, the legend pretty much ignored the fact that, of the four families represented by the original Pickering survivors, four different cultures were represented... and four different religions.

The survivors were:

A Hindu-practicing family of Indians, with the father, mother, and daughter;
One of the ship's cooks and his son, who practiced a combination of Confucianism, Buddhism, and Chinese folk religion;
A Moroccan merchant and his wife, who were Muslim;
And the Anglican Christian Robinson couple.

After subsequent births of the survivors and the children of their own intermarried children, what religion do you think the Puhni inhabitants were practicing when they were discovered?

Well, of course, the survivors' children and grandchildren were practicing an amalgam of all the religions, a religion that exists to this day, known as Puhnism.

So, what can we deduce from this?

Go ahead: stop reading for a moment, lift your eyes, and think about that question. What can we deduce from the fact that all these cultures and religious traditions combined to an amalgam??

Well, nothing, really.

It is true that there was a story called "The Swiss Family Robinson."

And Britain does have a Navy.

But everything else about the story is hogwash. I made it up. Even "malga root."

The very good reason I did so was to show that we all know impulsively the true nature of religion has to do with cultural identity and not some true or untrue claim to relevancy. Forced to live interdependently, people will naturally unify, and culture will alter religion- not the other way around.

The story makes sense.

I now go on to something that is the truth. Really.

Years ago, when I was fresh out of college, I worked at a Lutheran school in the Bronx teaching Junior High English. I was buddies with a fellow teacher, a much older gentleman, but one with whom I shared a Catholic upbringing. While riding the bus together, he enjoyed letting me know about all the projects in which he was active with the local church. I listened and supported him, never really letting on how fully I'd left Catholicism behind in my own life.

One day, we were discussing the ideals that all religions share, and with animation he described to me an interfaith program he was working on to create bridges between the Protestant religions and Catholicism with joint conferences, prayer groups, and community development projects. He hoped that in the future programs like this might lead to a unification of all Christian religions.

"Really!" I exclaimed. "What a remarkable idea!" I had no idea there were religious people who actually invested work in such a vision. And without another thought, I innocently asked, "And then, you could work on uniting with Judaism?"

The muscles in my friend's face dropped limp, his neck withdrew his head robotically, and, though he was looking away from me now, I could see his lips were mumbling over what was some other subject entirely.

I could feel the embarrassment-sent blood changing the color of my neck.

And, several years later, as a Probation Officer, I had a related experience. I shared a coffee break every morning with a veteran P.O., a tall, thin character with humored eyes. He'd grown up in Pittsburgh just before the Second World War, a Jewish kid in a very Christian culture.

It was Christmas time and I was feeling the warmth of the season (more in Chapter Eleven, "My Atheist Christmas,") humming "Hark, the Herald Angels Sing" with one elbow hooked over the edge of the doorway to his cubicle, sipping a cinnamon-laced coffee with the other hand. He smiled at my enthusiasm, but clearly was just plugging in another day at work, himself. I wanted to share the Christmas spirit with my friend, so I pursued him with a question:

"What I don't understand, Marvin, is how could you grow up in this country- in Pittsburgh of all places- and, regardless of your religion, not see Christmas as a special, heartwarming time of year?"

He thought about that, as he was a kind man, generous with his attention to such challenges from me. "Well, Marko," he told me, his fingers absent-mindedly running over the pre-sentence reports on his desk. "That wasn't something that included us. It was all around us, I know. But, it wasn't a warmth that reached into our world."

It is an idea that is very difficult to accept- that our experiences can be so vivid and moving, but still another person so close to us can be oblivious and untouched- as perplexing as unrequited love can be.

Of the moral changes that Religion has neglected to embrace, far and away the direst is the need to unify the world's people. It has failed miserably to unify.

Pulitzer Prize-winning entomologist, Edward O. Wilson informs, "Every tribe has a creation story... They can't be all right ... Religion... can talk about cooperation—interfaith activities. It can talk about virtue toward others and toward other groups... but then very quickly is transmogrified under stress into tribal aggression, the ancient instrument of human evolution brought back again."[63]

Since religion first became animated on Earth, there has never been a time when it has not exerted a significant divisive force among our world's people. None of the world's great tragic failures of tribal morality have occurred without religious collusion. And no religions have solved moral degeneration within their tribe.

Religious tribalism is not the carrying forth of a crucible of superior morality- rather, it is the barbarous, very conscious method through which we hold off inexorable change brought on by cross-tribal associations.

The distinctions people make in choosing a religion are not moral distinctions. Morally, most religions have similar

---

[63] In interview with NPR's Marty Moss-Coane on "Radio Times," April 24, 2012.

principles, loving ideals. No, like sports franchises, religions are differentiated by characters (players,) cultural identity (city,) symbols (logos,) dress (uniforms,) icons (mascots,) ritual (ie: the 11th-inning stretch, the national anthem, the manager's walk to the mound,) and stories (ie: the comeback kid, the unbroken streak, the desperation play...) These distinctions that have nothing to do with morality are what give religions definition away from other religions. Without these distinctions, and left just to morality, a universal ideal external to doctrine that churches have no control over, suddenly it would be too easy to lose control over what one's religion stands for- the meaning- the truth- the real truth. It would suddenly be too easy to lose control over the truth. No longer in the position of delivering the truth, one would be subject to its dictates of painful change (an excellent example being how the vast majority of US Catholics assert they use contraception, though the Church views it as a sin.)

If the truth is based on an ideal that is outside you, you are subject to its dictates, and you must change to remain valid. Religious tribes can only avoid change by claiming to control truth, glorifying our own stagnant state. The idea that any religious tribe has reached a stubborn perfection is absurd and narcissistic. We are, in fact, like cavemen to our descendants.

The security afforded us by knowing enough and not needing to know more, and to control the very limits of what might be known is of certain value, especially to the particularly insecure. But we only come alive from that experience that comes from outside us. Change is all life is. Not changing is not living. A religion that defends its integrity against change, seeks nothing.

That part of it that seeks to stay the same is dead.

Religions, purely cultural identities, do change. They must change. And the notion that they are settled or ideal or even proper is not only a poor view of the future, but a poor view of the past.

Tribalism has only one essential goal: to maintain a distinct identity, defensively. There is nothing spiritual about this goal. It is frightened, base, and slowly evolving into obscurity.

Chapter Nine
Scrooge's Gravestone

"Men's courses will foreshadow certain ends, to which, if persevered in, they must lead," said Scrooge. "But if the courses be departed from, the ends will change. Say it is thus with what you show me!"
The Spirit was immovable as ever.
Scrooge crept towards it, trembling as he went; and following the finger, read upon the stone of the neglected grave his own name, Ebenezer Scrooge.
"Am I that man who lay upon the bed?' he cried, upon his knees. The finger pointed from the grave to him, and back again. "No, Spirit! Oh no, no!"
The finger still was there.

In Stave IV of <u>A Christmas Carol</u>, Dickens has Scrooge being forced by the Ghost of Christmas Future to view his own gravestone. Scrooge has no choice but to make judgments on himself, the lesson being that to act without moral reflection is to cease to exist.

That is not the way real life seems to be. In real life, like a suicide bomber, one can sow misery and never be forced to face a reflective comeuppance. Men who dominated the world by running industries that filled the atmosphere and seas with toxins have already lived and died, never understanding a thing beyond success and wealth. The titans of mass murder have died perhaps without a touch of regret drawn from them for the intent of their horrid acts: Attila, Khan, Stalin, Hitler, Mao....

But then Dickens may answer that these men, having never lived morally, never really lived but the lives of zombies.

As for humanity, we have already survived long enough to see our own grave. The tombstone of modern humanity is the crystallization of corruptions so neglected that few of them are represented by words that contain starch enough to impart the meanings of them any longer. War, starvation, pollution, nuclear proliferation, poverty, greed... these are dead terms, used so much- apparent to us for so long- that they carry none of the import they need to.

Still, our progress does plod on. We cannot avoid making significant advances that come hand-in-hand with rising from bed. We change whether we like it or not.

Think about pop music. Why can't old recordings that were smash hits in prior generations be recycled on new generations of kids? It's not simply because they want to reject old things. Music is too impulsively engaging for that explanation to make sense. No, there's some kind of wisdom we pass down from one generation that the next one works on and advances.

This happens in other parts of our culture, too. Consider the civil rights advances of the Sixties. It wasn't that the vast majority population of Whites woke up one day cured of their corruption. And it wasn't that Black militancy frightened them into giving up their power. It was a moral contradiction that arose with the course of enlightenment, articulated intelligently by those visionaries, like Martin Luther King. Inexorably it spread. It is still spreading today into the tighter cultural crannies of the US landscape.

We advance just by showing up. Love and Truth cannot bear inconsistency. When called to our ideals, we can only resist change by resisting those ideals. That's what ideals are all about. They call the shots.

Those who wish to resist the changes called for by Truth can do so using tribally-inspired anti-intellectualism (think the "Drill-baby-drill" chants of the 2008 Republican Convention.) It takes more, though, to rally people to ignore the loving ideal than it does to get them to ignore the truth. To resist the changes called for by Love, some much more substantial tactic, like heavy-duty fear mongering, becomes necessary (think the demonization of immigrants or misrepresentation of the threats of foreign nations when we are ramping up to invade.)

My grandfather was a racist. I remember him watching the evening news in the Seventies and cursing at the video images of African Americans arguing for their liberty in Philadelphia, a city ruled by a mayor whose racial policies were disgraceful, who ran a black-booted police force off its leash, free to threaten, beat, and murder Blacks at will. My grandfather believed African Americans (he always used a different, vulgar term,) were lower forms of life, stupid and given to sinful excess. They needed to be controlled, or else they would corrupt our culture and destroy civilized ways of living. I'd add that he believed them to be impure. I'd say he thought they were germy, smelly- any of them, even famous people who stayed at fancy hotels with antiseptic bathrooms.

He probably believed their sweat was impure.

His harshest, most hateful words were always about Black people.

He came from a German family that had made their way onto US shores by opening a bakery in Philadelphia. He was the first US-born generation of our family, and as a man he did well with a successful banking career. Like most hard-striving cultures, his harsh side was not his only side. I'd have to say he was a very loving man. He loved his grandkids with all his heart and soul. Once when he was older, alone in a house caring for my Alzheimer-wasted grandmother, he sent me a Birthday card. It was one of those free cards old people get in offers to donate their money. Only it wasn't a birthday card, but just a photo of flowers that said "Hi!" with a blank inside. There, on his Underwood No. 5, he'd typed in the following:

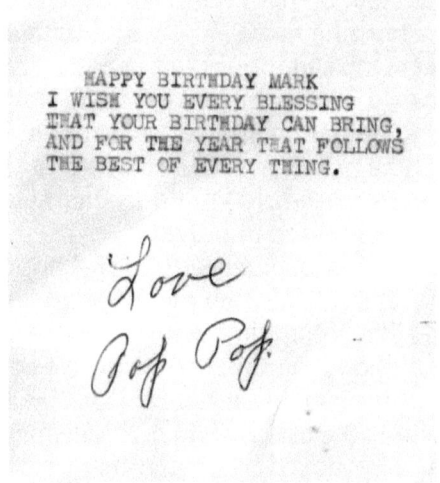

Once, about a year after my grandmother died, leaving Pop Pop a widower alone in their house a few blocks from the Jersey beach, my older brother, Bill, visited Atlantic City with an African-American girlfriend. Margate was nearby, and Bill decided to stop in and visit Pop Pop, accompanied by his steady. Surprised by Bill's evening visit, Pop Pop responded with graciousness and genuine warmth. He treated the young lady with nothing but tenderness and affection, and put the two of them up for the night as his guests.

To anyone who knew him, Pop Pop's behavior that night was incongruous with the way he always acted. In front of the television, in a voting booth, or even in church, he could find ways to get around the ideal of love, but, left no wiggle room, no way to avoid it, he had no choice but to behave in a loving way-the change was forced on him. He had no say when it came down to it.

We do not write the loving ideal; It writes us.

Our need for security in our way of life leads us to believe in constancy; that we do not improve and change as a species, that our children will do generally the same things we did and life will go on and on that way cheerily enough for us. If we were rather to view ourselves critically, understanding that the great moral changes ahead are imminent but simply unrecognized, we would be more compelled by our ideals, less tolerant of a lifestyle that seeks refuge in comfort.

Our inability to change at a pace that may meet our challenges in time is tied, then, to our desire to feel the comfort of security. There is nothing more hard-wired than a human creature seeking security. But it does not necessarily lead to a positive end. Our world is far removed from the state of nature where our minds and bodies could lead us through the most critical challenges. Like a deer who will run into the headlights of a car because in the natural world light only characterizes open space, we humans are plunging blindly.

Though we are closer than ever to a real popular awareness of justice, the world's rich and poor are as stratified as ever, 20% of the world's population using 80% of its resources. About 50% of all childhood deaths worldwide are attributed to malnutrition. 46% of Indian children under the age of 3 suffer from malnutrition and 16% are close to death despite the recent economic growth spurt enjoyed by the nation of 1.2 billion people.[64]

Further, our destructive capability over ourselves and over our ecology has recently expanded to no less than omnipotent. Though we more keenly understand the moral imperative of the loving ideal, our control over our own destructiveness is recklessly weak.

The victims of our ineptitude are everywhere:

Hawo, a girl 13 years old, born into a refugee camp, where she must stay to avoid being raped and murdered by human jackals that roam her countryside, soldiers who are inspired by religion, financed by international corporations you will find in your own pension fund who seek to profit off the development of Sudan's electrical grid, these soldiers themselves grown from innocent children victimized by human corruption. Hawo will perhaps live her entire life fleeing from one camp to another, never to breathe one free breath, as the decades ramble on without an international organization powerful enough to protect her.

Louisette, a 4-year-old Haitian child, who starved to death a month after being orphaned by the death of her mother, Isabella, a victim of cholera. These tragedies were caused by a lack of food and clean water in a country closer to Miami than Puerto Rico, just a hundred miles from "Hedonism," the Jamaican resort for "the inner child" of US tourists.

Dado, a 14-year-old boy of Rio De Janeiro, Brazil, one of many sex slaves trafficked on the beach by a man who carries boys' pictures in an album he offers to pedophile tourists. Or, Payal, of Mumbai, India, who, seeking housekeeping work after being abandoned by her husband, was abducted and forced into prostitution. Human sex trafficking is a crisis in nations all around the world,[65] but the attention to this issue by US foreign policy is no more than a sideline.

---

[64]For source/more info, see: http://www.unicef.org/india/children_2356.htm
[65]For source/more info, see:

Min, a young Chinese woman who lives on a shelf in a Shenzhen factory along with hundreds of other shelf-people co-workers, earning the equivalent of 45 cents an hour, as she assembles US toys 11 hours a day.

Azhar, an Iraqi mother who in 2003 was killed in an errant coalition missile attack that struck her home and also killed her husband, one of her sons, and 13 other members of her family. She was pregnant. Her other son, Ali, a 12 year old, was left alive but alone, and without both of his arms. As an adult, now, he tells the world, "My family were innocent farmers trying to live in peace."[66]

Piou, a 10-year-old Laotian girl, killed in 2010 by a US cluster bomb that had been dropped during the US's 1960's-era carpet-bombing of Vietnam. Her country is littered with such devices and to this day tragedies like hers occur regularly. The cluster bomb, originally a Nazi invention, is used to sprinkle smaller bombs that roll into hard-to-reach places. As these places are where civilians tend to hide, they are often the victims. According to the Nobel Peace Prize-laureat-agency, Handicap International, 27% of cluster bomb victims are children and 98% of cluster bomb victims are civilians.[67] Among the many civilians killed by the Minneapolis-made cluster bombs Israel dropped on Lebanon[68] during its 2006 bombing campaign was Hasaan, a 40-year-old father of three who was working to clear rubble several months later.[69]

---

http://en.wikipedia.org/wiki/Human_trafficking#United_States
[66] for more information, see:
http://www.timesonline.co.uk/tol/news/world/iraq/article6966523.ece
[67] For source/more info, see:
http://topics.nytimes.com/topics/reference/timestopics/subjects/c/cluster_munit
ions/index.html
[68] For source/more info, see:
http://www.thefreelibrary.com/The+use+of+cluster+munitions+in+the+war+o
n+terrorism.-a0179076804

Sasha, a 12-year-old US citizen, who remains with relatives, and who has not seen the mother she loves with all her heart for two years, since her mother was deported. She was deported because she had the audacity to leave the slums and misery of Ciudad Juarez, Mexico and cross the US border illegally in her search for a future with something more than her fate had assigned. The fact that her people have been pursuing migrant labor northward into the breadbasket of North America always, since before there even was such a thing as the USA, was of no import to the feds who sent her back.

...And let's not forget Felix, 22, who lives under a sheet-metal roof in the densely-populated slum where Sasha's mother has wound up, the slum he was born into and grew from a frightened child to a man in. He sits impatiently in wait for a van that will bring him to a place where he will attempt a desert crossing he has accomplished once before. He has a wad of bills in his front pocket. A bottle of salted water to keep him hydrated is in a knapsack beside the canvas door. At this moment, his wife smiles at him, as the baby is finally asleep.

Our world economy is based on the reinvestment of profit to spur new, expanded growth. Capitalism can do many things, but it cannot operate harmoniously with our planet. It must feed off of the digestion of new frontiers. Following the Great Depression, capitalism digested all the vast, unexploited frontiers of the world... until there were none left.

Having tapped all the oil wells on our lands[69], we finagled our way into the jungles of South America, spoiling them until they could yield no new profits. Then, we drilled in the seas.

---

[69] For source/more info, see:
http://www.bladepicturecompany.com/photojournale/details.php?image_id=1002

[70] Many forget this pursuit of oil began in Titusville, Pennsylvania, a relatively short time ago in the late 19th century. You can visit the town today and see its beaux arts mansions and public works, sponsored by the boom and thereafter preserved by the inertia left once the town dried up.

Having tapped those, we moved out to deeper sea. Some day we will run out.

That day may be soon. In 2006, oil prices shot up worldwide. Dire food shortages followed as food is conveyed around the world by oil-powered transportation and oil is essential to farming and modern fertilization. Tortilla riots saw Mexico into 2007. By 2008, news stories were focusing on the sales of cakes of mud among poor Haitians. More than a dozen countries experienced food riots. Later that year, the worldwide economy collapsed.

This rush to extract and use up the last of the world's oil and other fossil fuels is a competitive rush between nations to keep the capitalistic wheels spinning in a world desperate for sources of growth. It is a rush, at the same time, to fill the skies with fumes that will forever alter the natural ecological balance our lives have depended on. The logical human reaction to running out of oil should be to ration it and severely restrict our use of it. The logical capitalistic reaction is for each nation to ramp up its use of oil as quickly as possible, as oil allows industry and industry provides a competitive advantage. If China doesn't use all the oil it can, India will take up the slack. So, as we run out, the race becomes more heated, and we are actually consuming more. Much more.

Global fossil fuel emissions have increased by an average of over 3% a year since 2000 and the average is only ramping up, as every subsequent year breaks the record of the year that preceded it .

What has been progress for industrial capitalism has always been poison to its some. The short history of industrial capitalism is replete with exported bloodshed that has gone hand-in-hand with US progress: As the United States invaded Mexico under false pretenses; as we helped to overthrow the existing monarchy in Hawaii; as we seized Cuba, Puerto Rico, the Philippines, and Guam from Spain during the Spanish-American War; as the US intervened militarily in Nicaragua, Panama, Honduras, the Dominican Republic, Korea, Cuba, China, and Mexico, *all before* World War I; as we sent troops to Cuba, the Dominican Republic, Russia, Panama, Honduras, Yugoslavia, Guatemala, Turkey, and China *between* the world wars; as we engaged in a hundred additional military actions *following* World War II; from a time when all we needed to do was invade a nation or pay some cash to its unsophisticated leaders to make a profit, capitalism, always pretty filthy, became consistently filthier to the point now where international corporations desperate for their next sources of growth compete to be the first to do business directly with murderous regimes[71]. The second a murderous dictator has wiped the blood off his hands he goes from pariah to dealmaker, a bright opportunity for a lucky corporation's new telecommunications or electrical gridding contracts. Morality just does not exist.

In these austere times, after capitalism has profited from downsizing and the vast destruction of unions; by the absorption of homemakers into the workforce while cutting salaries and benefits so as to make necessary the dual-income family; by the shifting of jobs to more desperate regions of the world, so as, through competition, to drag down our standard of living; this hungry beast has turned to its last scoundrelous refuge: debt. By raising worldwide debt, the rich can continue to spoon themselves profits- servings, of course, swiped off the plates of future generations.

Meanwhile, every year of the past 6 years has scored a higher average temperature on our planet than any year since measurements were begun in 1880.[72] Due in part to the depletion of non-renewable aquifers, USAID estimates that by 2025 one-third of the world's people will face severe and chronic water shortages, which has dire implications for food production and disease prevention.[73] Seas of floating plastic trash, one of which is twice the size of Texas, continue to grow in the middle of the Pacific.[74] Due to a variety of factors caused by humans, especially deforestation, in the lifetime of a child born today, half of all plant and animal species can be expected to be extinct.[75]

In his insightful book, The Black Swan, Nicholas Taleb[76] criticizes modern economic critiques by comparing their logic to

---

[71] For source/more info, see:
http://www.state.ct.us/.../corporate%20social%20responsibility%20in%20genc idal%20regions.ppt

[72] For source/more info, see: http://blog.sustainablog.org/2010-global-average-temperature/

[73] For source/more info, see:
http://www.usaid.gov/our_work/environment/water/water_crisis.html
http://www.unesdoc.unesco.org/images/0014/001469/146997e.pdf

[74] For source/more info, see:
http://www.dailygalaxy.com/my_weblog/2007/12/are-there-reall.html

[75] For source/more info, see:
http://raysweb.net/specialplaces/pages/Wilson.html

[76] Taleb, N. N., (2007) The Black Swan: The Impact of the Highly

that of a turkey waddling confidently out of his hutch on Thanksgiving morning, expecting to find the food he has been feeding off every morning of his life- the food he feels he has all rights to expect- though his expectation is entirely, foolishly wrong.

Taleb's turkey is oblivious, but those who steer our economy have all the knowledge of the world at their fingertips. Then, I ask, should the modern economist be condemned for purposely ignoring the consequences?

The answer is that the modern world controlled by power elites is steered with reference to the frame of myriad layers of human-devised constructs- not the true state of nature. An effort to see the world as it really is- without constructs- would leave the modern economist with no knowledge. Go ahead, ask an economist whether we really should be ingesting resources that are not renewable or whether we should be borrowing from our children, and that economist will be the first to tell you the question is out of their purview, that, instead, they are there to tell you whether or not it is likely to succeed in its purpose, the means that will be most effective, the likely outcomes, etc... And then, they may tell you to ask the one who has authority over such questions, your pastor.

A hundred years ago, we had a primitive view of our place in the world. We did not contemplate beyond our purview, foolishly assuming there were no boundaries we might outgrow. We were not responsible for the morality of the clockwork of our world, as it was not within our grasp.

Now, we are many times more clearly in control of the world's resources, but we still act without any responsibility to manage the world's consumption. Ignoring current and impending failure, we self-destructively pursue growth with the magical turkey-thinking that something that brought progress in the past always can be counted on to eventually work out.

Rather, the thinking of creative morality is built upon the ironclad core of love- that firm ideal that, unlike a construct invented by us, firmly dictates and so invents us. We find the proper place where we belong in the future, and then we look back scornfully on our current ways. Then, we chart a course in the direction that leads towards the way of the natural, loving ideal.

Improbable, Random House.

The view takes the control of our decisions out of the influence of our insecure hungers and desires and gives responsibility for that control to our ideals. The view calls it cowardice to be unwilling to lose that hunger-motivated control- to be unwilling to give up our security to the control of the loving ideal.

The cowardice that resists idealistic change ranges from the condemnation of change as evil to mournfully declaring change impossible. This cowardice is rooted in the moral failure of greed, which is an intimate of insecurity, a basic primitive human motivation.

On April 18, 1977, President Jimmy Carter addressed the nation about the growing crisis brought on by the results of our nation's profligate energy policies. The speech began like this:

> *Tonight I want to have an unpleasant talk with you about a problem unprecedented in our history. With the exception of preventing war, this is the greatest challenge our country will face during our lifetimes. The energy crisis has not yet overwhelmed us, but it will if we do not act quickly.*
> *It is a problem we will not solve in the next few years, and it is likely to get progressively worse through the rest of this century.*
> *We must not be selfish or timid if we hope to have a decent world for our children and grandchildren.*
> *We simply must balance our demand for energy with our rapidly shrinking resources. By acting now, we can control our future instead of letting the future control us...[77]*

Two years later, Carter delivered his famous "malaise" speech where he called on citizens to control their energy usage and Congress to grant him mandatory control of energy consumption. The next year, he was voted out of office.

During Carter's administration, payrolls and benefits were still union-strong, almost half of the nation's families only contributed one parent to the job force, and the government taxed enough to control debt.

The presidents since Carter have skyrocketed the national debt.[78] The US worker is now a landslide of concessions away from that comparatively idyllic 1970's. The concessions promise to continue, and every year we receive less- from our government, our institutions, and our employers.

My hope is for us to reach a new generation that is capable of a global rethink- a rejection of competitive nationalism, (morality is universal- not American or Western,) an impulse towards industry that is holistically meaningful, and an intolerance for all that is unloving.

We may reach a point where a new realization wakes the enthusiastic child that sleeps in the mind of the selfish old man.

The answer will not be in our failure, a new society rising from our ashes. Mining Watch Canada reports there are 217,000 toxic waste areas in the US alone that require perpetual care, so it can be assumed that if we fail only a perpetually poisonous world will result.

And he turns to the ghost and asks if one last chance is still possible.

To a person who lives with hope, we have arrived at a point beyond which everything conventional is unsustainable, so that a drastic change to a better way is not only possible, but mandated.

We must change.

And that is very good news.

---

[77] For source/more info, see:
http://millercenter.org/scripps/archive/speeches/detail/3398
[78] For source/more info, see:
http://en.wikipedia.org/wiki/National_debt_by_U.S._presidential_terms

Chapter Ten
An Atheist's Christmas

To be what you must, you must give up what you are.
-Yusuf Islam,[79] (formerly, Cat Stevens.)

You might wonder why an atheist buys a Christmas tree. You might be puzzled to find a cheerful Christmas card from me. If you were to see me in my home, you'd be well within your rights to accuse, "What the heck are you doing singing "Deck the Halls" and mixing up eggnog, you bleeping atheist?!"

In our home growing up, Christmas was the most special holiday of the year. It wasn't just the presents. It was the music, the food, the good cheer. The Grinch and Charlie Brown on television. Of course, the streets of my Pennsylvania hometown bustled with happy people wishing you merry, while the wind blew cold and the dark fell early. Tinny music streaming from State Street. Maybe you can relate.

Even midnight mass. It was the one mass of the year that promised not to be martyrizingly boring. One tender or cheerful song after another, everyone singing, everyone in fine spirits. What's not to love?

And then, the story. Well, we never knew the real Biblical story of Christmas. Probably no one at a modern midnight mass does, either. No, modern Americans have developed a story that suits us mythically, even though it is full of details not mentioned in the Bible or even in conflict with the Bible- or which are represented in none of the early Biblical sources.[80]

The fantastic story we told went as follows: A poor man and his pregnant, but virgin, wife are wandering and hungry. They bed down for the night on the straw of a cattle stall, and she gives birth to a beautiful baby boy. At the same time, a bright star

---

[79] This is a lyric from "To Be What You Must," by Yusuf Islam.
[80] The early sources have the most claim to relevance, as, in the age of Christ, when everything came from very unreliable spoken word traditions, the farther a source gets from an event in time, the more ridiculous the account becomes (think about that children's game where a secret is whispered from one ear to the next.) That said, the first of these stories came a good 35 years after Christ's life ended and (though they contained alleged quotes,) in a different language than Christ spoke, so that even the early sources require a large scoop of faith to purchase. See http://en.wikipedia.org/wiki/Gospel_of_Mark.

bursts to life in the sky directly overhead. Far and wide, angels appear, telling of a new child that has been born- a child who will lead the world to peace. Kings, seeking guidance, follow the star, bringing their finest gifts. The story ends with the great kings on their knees before this child, acknowledging the greatness that will arise from this ignoble station. And the animals speak.

It is appealing to modern Americans in the same way the Horatio Alger stories were. I still love our Nativity story. It tells that the true meaning of life has nothing to do with cash and flashy cars and power over others. The most virtuous of us will be vulnerable and broke. It is the love that guides us that brings virtue. It is our selflessness.

So, I tell this story to my kids.

Of course I do.

I buy a tree. We deck it with balls and garlands and lights, just the way my Christian forebears did, just the way my ancient Irish and German Pagan ancestors would've done if they'd had electricity thousands of years ago, the tree being one of the Pagan traditions Christians incorporated to encourage Pagans to become Christianized. (If they'd incorporated mound-building, too, I guess we'd all have red and green shovels stored up on our top front closet shelves, right?)

I play carols on my guitar for my kids before bed. When my 4-year-old asks what "say your prayers" means in the song, "Here comes Santa Claus," I tell her, "Well, some people believe there is a person who lives in the sky who created everything, and they like to talk to him quietly before they go to bed." I add, to explain better, that I don't believe in the creator person. Testing me, her eyes sparkle, and she says, "I do." I give her a warm smile and switch the lights off.

It's fine with me. We had much the same conversation about Santa the month before, as we walked home from the Thanksgiving parade.

It's not indoctrination. It's just story fun. My children have not been denied any knowledge, and no one ever told them they needed to believe in any particular story or that they'd be good to believe this or bad to believe that.

Christmas gives me an opportunity to (clumsily) reassemble for my children many healthy cultural elements traditionally provided by religion. I can no more call attention to religion's failures than I must acknowledge the vital role it has played and often still does in our culture. Beyond being the sole instructor of morality beyond the family, religion provides great comfort to the lonely and disturbed. It has been the source of our cultural richness, being our crucible for tradition, community, social service, political action, leadership, social union, song, stories, symbols... - ritual and safe haven, even. And inspiration.

As an atheist, I can tell you from first-hand experience that that cultural richness can be reassembled to much success outside a religion, but I also can see clearly that it doesn't need to be just one or the other. Just like the Christians and Pagans did, just as the shipwreck victims did in the lie I told about the Swiss Family Robinson, we can share our lives, our stories, our cultures, and even our beliefs. We can nurture our community in an inclusive way and still be separate people with original ideas.

To create the real change that our fate demands of us, we must be different than we have been for the past several thousand years. We must think in ways we haven't before. We must change.

This means breaking through devices such as the absolutist purity-evil dualism and the strict identities that define our religions and organize our worldwide family into enemy factions. These devices stifle nuanced critique and intellectual debate of problems we need to instead become more intimate with in order to work together to found solutions for.

While I was trying to focus on a fix-it project this morning, my 7-year-old daughter, from across the den near the hamster cage, excitedly cried out, "Daddy, look! I see Brownie walking through his tube to his other cage!"

Any parent can attest young kids are always exclaiming, "Look!" with reference to unremarkable things to see. It is a parent's most routine and tedious challenge to summon the appropriate mirroring interest.

Though we may roll our eyes at the child, it is the child, here, whose mind is more active.

When we are children, time passes quite slowly. A year is a very long time. As we get older, we find our experience of time seems to shorten considerably. Whole years seem to fly by. "It seems it was just yesterday..." adults begin, with one another, and the other is already nodding in agreement.

The difference in impressions seems to be due to the novel nature of the experience rather than the difference in age of the person who is experiencing time.[81] Novel or new experiences attract more of our attention.

---

[81] Listen to Robert Krulwich's marvelous NPR radio essay at:

A walk down a street to a grown-up is filled with details we have learned not to pay any attention to: the expressions on the faces of fellow pedestrians, the color of the leaves on the trees, the way the ants gather in a hole at the curb... Children notice all these things, and their minds work on each of them. Their days are very long. They simply have more experiences.

And so it is that the quality of our living, in essence, may very well be attributed to novelty, to change. To live a routine may be seen to some extent a zombie life. It is as if the difference, the learning, the growth, accounts for the richness of life entirely, and that the routine is empty. To live the richest life would be to change everything you can, to try to always be critical of your own security, to notice everything you can.

It reminds me of the imperative of the popular Philadelphia psychologist Dan Gottlieb to "wake up every time you walk through a doorway," or that of the 17th Century nun, St. Teresa of Avila, to "do whatever most kindles love in you," which is a sort of constant reimagining of oneself under the guidance of the loving ideal.

When I do this, when I ditch routine and reimagine the current experience of life, when I "wake up" or test my own sense of what kindles love in me, in wonder, I look at my children, amazed that they are mine.

This experience runs counter to earlier impressions I've had of my life where I saw myself as driving my world- causing it. For once, the moment is not somewhere on the road ahead. The moment is NOW.

When religious leaders demand faithful adoration, devotion, and reverence, people of all religions and atheists alike need only respond with a committed practice of our loving ideals now here on Earth, not only decrying moral corruption but also soundly rejecting it. A.J. Muste a political activist said- "There is no way to peace; peace is the way." [82] The quote is often misattributed to Gandhi because it understands that only the practice of our ideals brings them about. The minute we practice our ideals in response to our religion; adoration, devotion, and

---

http://www.npr.org/templates/story/story.php?storyId=122322542

[82] As quoted in The New York Times, (16 November 1967.) Another great Muste quote: When a reporter asked him if he thought his stoic protest in front of the White House through wind and rain would change the country's Vietnam policies, Muste replied: "Oh, you've got it all wrong. I'm not doing this to change the country. I do it so the country won't change me."

reverence are transformed from a self-obsessed, aspirational demonstration for God to a selfless expression of our loving ideals- of our dignity.

"Grace," I think it's called.

Swarthmore, PA, 1983: Returning from college over the winter break, I stepped off the train into a heavy snowfall. My parents weren't expecting me, and I decided to make my own way home with my duffel bag slung over my shoulder, rather than calling for a ride.

I was a student on a course towards various professional goals, but they meant really nothing to me at the time. I was in love- a glorious, swooning, unrequited love of the type college students often find themselves lost in- almost a state of being in love with being in love- the egocentrism of the teenaged years yielding to a just-as-obsessed focus on someone outside who mirrors oneself.

I remember when I first watched her across the lunch table as she did something I did. I forget what- some affectation of mine- she did it, and I was awed because it was clear she was welcoming me intimately.

I was strongly idealistic, as, of course, is not unusual in college. Young adults made secure by the role of student, living fairly independently, and encouraged to question their place in life freely, will choose the generosity and fellowship of idealism. Only after college, when they must begin scrapping for their survival, can competition and material aspiration settle them into ruts with ends that are selfish, cowardly, and uninspired.

A long lawn across the campus of Swarthmore College was the shortcut I usually took. The previous summer I walked my dog there every night. She chased rabbits with passion, but was never able to get closer than a nip at their heels. The old brick buildings and ancient shade trees, overhung now with a moss of snow rather than leaves, listened silently to my high-top sneaker footfalls in the deep pile.

My spirit was immensely strong.

I finished with the lawn and stepped up onto the sidewalk at the residential area on the opposite end of the campus. Houses looking across at each other were lit, and some had colored lights in the windows, but I was alone on the street.

I made my footing carefully down a steep, snaking lane, and left that neighborhood behind me. Meeting the deepest snow at the base of the hill, it took me longest to advance through a block-long section of street bordered by undeveloped, rocky creekland before my parent's house came into sight.

Past their old clunker of a car and up the short hill, I heard my father's voice first through the kitchen window above. He spoke easily so I knew he'd been drinking. But his words were strung tightly enough that I could tell he wasn't yet in his cups. The tinny radio had Bing Crosby softly barking, "Oh Come, All Ye Faithful."

I stepped softly on the wooden steps as I climbed up to the back porch.

I was thrilled to take the doorknob in my hand.

I had a loving place in my world. It was built from essentially my mother's thin paycheck as a parochial school teacher. As little as we had, it amounted to all a person should ever really need. An artist could take that place and make it into anything at all. It is a very simple thing to achieve, after which every other effort can be extended generously outward.

Surely, all children deserve to have food, medical care, shelter, and education, enough to fund a modest lifetime of hope. And no grown man or woman on Earth should be kicking back with more until that basic task has been taken care of.

If not, what good are we, really? What are we worth?

And, why is there such a big difference between children and grown-ups? If a child should have the right to a small bit of hope, why shouldn't the child's father or grandmother? Do we become less worthy the longer we live? Or is it just easier to ignore the humanity of a person who has lost their baby-fat cheeks and has become hardened by their loss of innocence?

Recently, I was listening to a radio show, where a conservative newspaper columnist was asked if, rather than just tearing down President Obama's health care plan, he had any health plan of his own to put forward. His answer was startlingly honest:

> I don't believe that the United States tradition is that we should supply everything everybody needs or wants. That's not the American form of government. I think we should expedite market forces and provide some targeted subsidies to give a reasonable chance for most people to get care, but the idea that we are going to be able to provide this post-World War II fantasy, which is falling apart in Europe now, and we're now trying

to walk towards the fantasy, is crazy because we
can't afford it...
We had an illusion after World War II that we
could- we could provide everything for everybody,
and we now have riots in the streets throughout
Western Europe because we can't do it, and we're
trying to step back to reality, and America needs
to recognize that reality. [83]

The idea that the world's economic forces are creating our
future at the cost of our very ability to provide basic health care is
an absurd capitulation of our moral responsibility. The gall of
one of us to condemn the less fortunate to misery while he sits
secure in modern comforts is a rejection of the notion of
community, what is basic to the loving ideal, formed at a parent's
warm embrace.

But this is not a question of mere generosity. The step
away from selfishness and towards community for this radio
commentator would not be as easy as tossing change to a beggar.
In fact, it would be a step away from an entire way of living.

He will not change.

Others will, though.

No matter how sheepish citizens would like to claim their
role is in their religion, religious devotion is an act of commission
or omission that all people must hold themselves accountable
for. A universal moral standard for humanity exists. I refer to it
here as the ideal of love. That standard is our rule for
accountability.

A deep flaw of our society has been its inability to
articulate this ideal in secular moral standards, and to apply and
instruct them to its citizens. Morality must find a strong place in
the civic sphere. It must form our civic and political decisions,
guided by our vision of the morally glorious developments ahead.
The first step towards imagining our moral advancement is
acknowledging it and disengaging from servility to the codes of
our primitive forefathers.

Taking care of me, fulfilling my needs, serving solely
myself is expected, the first thing I seek to do. There is nothing

[83] The comment is by Tony Blankley, columnist for the Washington Times,
from the 1/7/2011 episode of "Left, Right, and Center," a political talk show of
KCRW, a Santa Monica College public radio station. Mr. Blankley has
subsequently passed away.

virtuous about it. Virtue is less primal, more highly developed. Virtue requires work and sacrifice of one's own very egoistic impulse. Morality is selfless, and is always focused outside me. Morality threatens radical change to every construct that comforts us.

Biologist, J. B. S. Haldane, warns us, "The thing that has not been is the thing that shall be... no beliefs, no values, no institutions are safe."

Love is principled. We have no control over the demands of love. Justice lives in the heart of love.